NAVY SURGEON: VIETNAM

by William J. Walsh, M.D.

DORRANCE
PUBLISHING CO
EST. 1920
PITTSBURGH, PENNSYLVANIA 15238

Dorrance Publishing Co
585 Alpha Drive
Pittsburgh, PA 15238
Visit our website at *www.dorrancebookstore.com*

ISBN: 978-1-6491-3457-8
eISBN: 978-1-6491-3810-1

This publication is dedicated to the over seven hundred patients that it was my privilege to care for during 1966 and 1967 while serving on the hospital ship USS Repose in the Republic of Vietnam.

ACKNOWLEDGMENTS

I must recognize the hospital personnel of the USS Repose, the doctors, nurses, corpsmen, and technicians whose selfless dedication and professionalism resulted in the awarding of the Naval Unit Citation for producing a survival rate of more than 99% in our patients, the best record in treating military casualties up until that time. The officers and crew of the ship were also admirable for providing a safe and comfortable environment for our patients to recover in. I especially wish to recognize the members of the Surgery Service that it was my pleasure to work with, especially Captain William Snyder, Commander Larry Glass, Lieutenant Commander Rod McDonald, Lieutenant Gerry Verdi, and Lieutenant Royce Hansen. These men assisted me, taught me, and inspired me.

I am grateful for the many individuals that were willing to share their stories with me during my year in Vietnam. These stories are still with me after fifty years.

In twenty-fifteen I returned to the areas in Vietnam where I had been and where my patients had been wounded on a Vietnam Battlefield Tour. The tour group consisted of veterans who had served in the Northern I Corps Region and was led by Marine Sergeant Bill Stilwagon. The tour was very helpful to me in understanding Vietnam during the conflict and at the present time. Bill Stilwagon was a very efficient leader and teacher and he remains a friend. Members of the group shared their stories of Vietnam and their tears. It was a good experience, but not an easy one.

My writing has benefitted from participation in the Veterans Writing Group at Fordham University under the direction of David Surface. I have been inspired by all of the veterans in the group, the majority having served in Vietnam.

My family has played a big role in my becoming a surgeon and a writer. My parents gave me the encouragement to persevere. Through the long years of medical education. My brothers and sisters have been very supportive of my late start as a writer. My wonderful wife, Melinda has succeeded in making my writing and everything in my life better.

CONTENTS

CHANGE OF PLANS

I had been summoned to meet with the chairman of surgery at St. Vincent's Hospital on an afternoon in early April, 1966. I was not surprised by the call. I had been expecting it. I had applied for a position of second year surgical resident and had been confidently awaiting a call to confirm I had been accepted for the position. The St Vincent's surgical residency was a pyramid program that started with eight residents and would finish after five years with two chief residents. Residents had to re-apply each year for a position the following year. It was like playing "musical chairs." My work had been good and I felt certain of being promoted.

The chairman, Dr. Louis Rousellot, was an extraordinary man. He was brilliant, an excellent surgeon, and an exceptional teacher. He had developed surgical procedures that were used worldwide. He had the most skillful hands I had ever seen in a surgeon, and he required the same kind of skill from his residents. He was also a very demanding chief, not tolerating poor performance in his staff. On occasion, he would fire a resident on the spot for making a bad decision. He never lost his temper or shouted; his speech was quiet and controlled, but what he said was the word and could not be challenged.

I walked into the chief's office and was seated. Dr. Rousellot did not waste any words. In a firm voice, he said, "Dr. Walsh, you have applied for a resident position next year. I cannot give it to you. The war in Vietnam is expanding and the military will need doctors. You have no deferment and you will be drafted. I do not want any resident drafted out of my program. I can promise you a position after you have completed your military obligation."

That was it. His message was a total shock.

I walked out of the office and paused to digest what I had just been told. I realized I was about to become unemployed. Furthermore, I was probably unemployable as other surgical programs would not hire a resident with my draft status. On graduating from medical school, male physicians had to decide what to do about military service. The government offered the "Berry Plan" which allowed doctors to complete internship or residency, and then serve in the military. I chose not to join the Berry Plan as doctors were not being drafted at that time. I had a goal to finish residency in surgery and then to complete two additional years or fellowship in cardiac surgery, followed by going into practice as a heart surgeon. Vietnam changed everything! My plans had to change.

I paused briefly and the resumed walking. I walked out of the hospital and then three blocks north on 7th Avenue to the nearest Navy recruiting office where I was warmly greeted. The Navy would be happy to have me. I asked where I would be stationed. The recruiting officer suggested I visit the office in Washington where all the doctors got their duty station assignments.

The next week, I took the train to Washington and a cab to Navy headquarters there. The man I had to see was a doctor about my age and wearing civilian clothes. He immediately informed me I would likely be sent to Vietnam, either with the Marines or on a hospital ship. He added that I could request an aircraft carrier in the Mediterranean. I fell for the bait and inquired about the carrier. He smiled and told me there was no such option. Anyone requesting the carrier would be sent to the Marines. I chose to go to the hospital ship, USS Repose, and I never regretted the choice.

WELCOME ABOARD

I n the summer of 1966, things were happening rapidly. Having completed all the necessary documentation, a letter arrived from the Navy indicating that I was being commissioned with the rank of lieutenant. I was sworn in, vowing to defend the Constitution of the United States of America. The following day, I drove to a Navy supply store in Brooklyn to purchase a set of uniforms. The next day, donning my new uniforms, I showed up at St. Albans Navy Hospital in Queens for my introduction into the service. I don't recall if my uniform was on properly or not. My processing passed for what was my basic training. It was a rush job of preparing a civilian surgeon on his way to the war. There was no marching or push-ups. It was just me and a chief petty officer in a small, drab room. I practiced a proper salute a few times, had my placement of rank insignia corrected, heard a few words to the effect that I was a doctor and no one expected me to act too military.

Mostly I watched movies about the Navy. Some of the films were too dull to take seriously (e.g. "the Organization Structure of Navy Command") that I turned away out of boredom. Others were too scary (e.g. "How to Establish an Aid Station Under Enemy Fire") that was too disturbing to watch. There was one film that did get my attention. It was called "Procedure for Boarding a United States Navy Ship." The topic seamed useful as I expected to be boarding my ship, the USS Repose, in a short time. I was anxious to make a good impression on my ship and felt that it was important to follow proper protocol in coming aboard. The film showed a handsome young officer in crisply starched dress-white uniform ascending the gangplank, pausing before stepping onto the deck and crisply saluting the ensign and the officer of the deck and, in perfect tone asking, "Permission to come aboard." I memorized the act and determined I would board the Repose in exactly that way. I didn't feel like I was a real Navy officer, but I felt like I could do an impersonation of one.

In between movies, I was sent off to other assignments, including medical and dental exams. Heading to Southeast Asia, I required multiple inoculations for a large number of the world's diseases, about sixteen in all. These had to be administered separately for reasons of comfort and safety. I was also sent to see a lawyer to complete my Last Will and Testament. All of this took two days, separated by a weekend off. Then I was the summoned to the office of the commanding officer, where I received travel orders to the USS Repose.

After a long and complicated trip, I awoke in the Da Nang Bachelor Officer Quarters. A chief petty officer wearing fatigues entered my room and told me to get my gear and come with him to the airfield to fly to Dong Ha where the USS Repose was operating. I boarded a C-130 with an ensign, who was also going to the Repose. Our instructions were to exit the plane immediately after landing. The aircraft would land, taxi, and then? immediately take-off. The huge rear door of the C-130 opened and the crew chief heaved my luggage out onto the field and urged me to follow it out. It was a short leap to the turf. Looking around, there was no sign of my ship or of any water. The young ensign and I were in the middle of a large, flat field. Spotting a group of Marines, I enquired about how to get to the USS Repose. They pointed to an area where the wounded were being assembled to be transported to the hospital ship. We joined the group and, shortly two UH-34 helicopters appeared and loading began.

We were quickly flying over the coast and a beautiful white ship could be seen in front of us. I was reviewing my instructions for ship boarding, but I wasn't sure how the process would work, exiting a helicopter. The chopper landed on the little flight deck. I watched as the man ahead of me jumped to the deck, ducked his head below the whirling helicopter blade and scurried out of the way. I followed him and copied his exit. I found myself walking down the ramp to the triage area where I was greeted by several officers who were asking if I was their replacement. I had no answer I could give. I stopped and realized I had not saluted the ensign or the officer of the deck and I had not asked anyone for permission to come aboard. However, I had gotten on board without embarrassing myself. I felt like I had just officially joined the Navy.

FLIGHT QUARTERS

Flight Quarters! The call rang out throughout the ship. Crew members on deck could already see six UH-34 helicopters coming across the sky, looking like a procession of ants.

"All hands, man your flight quarter stations! Litter bearers, lay up to the flight deck on the double! All hands prepare to receive thirty emergency medivacs!"

This last announcement was followed by a collective "Oh shit" by the entire ship's company.

I hurried to the triage area. Helicopters were circling to land. The crash boat with divers was lowered into the water. Corpsmen were at the flight deck, ready to carry the wounded to triage. In triage, the medical staff worked earnestly to evaluate the extent of wounds on each patient. The wounded Marines were silent, never complaining or crying out in pain from their horrible injuries. It's hard to imagine their discipline.

After triage, I headed to the operating room, changed into a scrub suit, and checked on our first patient of the day. My partners, Commander Larry Glass and Lieutenant Gerry Verdi, were setting up in operating room two. Our first patient was a penetrating gunshot wound of the abdomen. Two loops of bowel required repair, but all went well. I scrubbed out to the prep area to ready our next patient for the O.R.

As I entered the prep room, out of the corner of my eye, I saw a corpsman from another surgical team preparing a patient for surgery, a Marine who had a leg shattered by a mine and was scheduled to have an amputation. The corpsman, seeing me, called out franticly, "Dr. Walsh!" I immediately saw the cause for panic. A clot had dislodged from the femoral artery and a frightening stream of pulsatile blood was exiting from his thigh wound, shooting across the room, and splashing on the far bulkhead! Both the corpsman and the Marine showed abject panic in their faces.

The corpsman had been shaving the thigh with a straight razor. When the bleeding suddenly opened, he tried to stop it using a large clamp, but there was so much shredded tissue around the vessel that he was unable to accurately clamp it. The frightening hemorrhage continued.

I grasped the patient's ankle with my left hand and raised the leg. I could see that it was attached to the body by a small mass of skin, ligaments, and muscle. I took the straight razor from the corpsman and swung it in a big arc across the thigh, severing it. Then I handed the leg to the shocked corpsman who nearly fainted. With the limb out of the way, the femoral artery was clearly visible and was easily clamped, stopping the hemorrhage.

My recollection is that my whole involvement in this matter took about one minute. The corpsman rallied from his shock. I turned to the marine to offer words of encouragement. He faced me and, before I could say a word, he looked me in the eye and quietly said:

"Thank you, sir."

I wasn't able to keep track of the marine after that day. I don't even know his name. But I will never forget him.

HANNIBAL AND HIS ANIMALS

L CMDR Donald Hannibal was the radiologist on the USS Repose. He was a good radiologist, hard-working, intelligent, and thoughtful. He was handsome in a Midwestern, wholesome sort of way. He was slender and fit-looking with a square jaw and wirerimmed glasses. He was the only radiologist on board, so he was on call twenty-four hours a day, every day. Donald Hannibal was Regular Navy, a carrier Navy doctor. Strangely, he had one physical problem that a career Navy person should not have. He was prone to sea-sickness. In heavy seas, he could not sit or stand to read X-rays without feeling ill. He handled this by lying flat on his back on an X-ray table and holding the films up to an overhead light to read them. He did what he had to do to get the job done.

I recall one case where Hannibal's attention to detail relieved my confusion. I was preparing a wounded Marine for surgery. He had been shot in his leg and the bullet had shattered his tibia. I was reviewing his X-ray films to plan fracture repair. There were a number of bone fragments, but they didn't seem as if they would go together properly. Dr. Hannibal carefully reviewed the films and concluded that one piece of bone did not seem to come from this tibia. I went back to the Marine and asked if anyone had been next to him when he was hit. He answered that his buddy was with him and that the same bullet also went through his leg. His buddy had been flown to a different hospital and we were unable to return that bone fragment to its rightful owner.

Dr. Hannibal was assisted in his department by six radiology technicians, who called themselves "Hannibal's animals." They distinguished themselves by their unique uniforms. The "animals" all wore blue jeans and white tee shirts. The shirts were labeled in front with bold lettering, stating "HANNI-BAL'S ANIMALS." They also sported identical mustaches. The result was a group of guys, looking as if they'd been cloned from a prototype. They were a happy band of X-ray warriors. They labored day and night delivering a high level of radiologic performance.

One evening, when the entire hospital was reeling from overwork, I was in the radiology area with several new patients at three a.m. and one of the animals called his boss, saying, "Dr. Hannibal, we have thirteen new patients in the department." Not hearing a response, he repeated, "Dr. Hannibal!" Turning around, the tech saw Dr. Hannibal standing behind him, saying, "Let's go to work!" Hannibal had saved time by skipping the bother of dressing; he was standing in boxer shorts and a tee shirt.

The LCMDR was frequently lost in thought. Sometimes his thoughts were peculiar. He was very worried about the USS Repose sinking. This was not entirely abstract. The USS Comfort, another hospital ship, during the Korean conflict collided with an oiler and sank in fourteen minutes. The fastest time for the USS Repose in an abandon ship drill had been fourteen minutes. At every drill, Dr. Hannibal was in the lifeboats first, his lifejacket on and ready to go. He gave careful thought to how an enemy would sink the ship and he concluded that it would be by torpedo. I'm not sure how he thought that this torpedo would be launched but he was certain it would be aimed at the engine room and that the torpedo path would pass through his compartment and through the lower bunk. He, therefore, insisted on taking the upper bunk.

Fortunately, we were never torpedoed. However, like the USS Comfort, we did collide with an oiler. The USS Repose sustained major damage, including a large hole in the hull. The alarm sounded for general quarters. Damage Control was called to action. There was understandable excitement everywhere. I was busy finishing my surgery as quickly as possible. I didn't know what Hannibal was doing at this time, but I wouldn't be surprised if he was sitting in a lifeboat wearing a lifejacket and underwear, waiting for "Abandon ship!" to be called.

MURPHY

L et me tell you about Murphy. In one year in Vietnam, I met a lot of characters, but none were as colorful or as confounding as Murphy. I used his surname because no one seemed to know his given name or his rank. I would surmise that Murphy was a major in the US Air Force. I can't say for certain because he never wore a uniform. I believe that he was the biggest rule breaker in Vietnam. In reality, he made his own rules.

One day I responded to the call for Flight Quarters. A Marine UH-34 helicopter landed on the flight deck with an unusual cargo. Instead of the usual group of casualties, a tall Irish guy swaggered down the ramp to the triage area followed by six Vietnamese civilians. In triage, the Irish guy announced that he was Dr. Murphy, a surgeon from the Cam Ran Bay Air Force Hospital, and he had with him six patients needing heart surgery. Captain Snyder Chief of Surgery and an excellent cardiac surgeon handled the situation smoothly and quickly.

The USS Repose had the only heart surgery team in Vietnam and Murphy wanted to work with our team. The six patients were admitted to the "International Ward" to be evaluated and prepared for open heart surgery. Murphy was given a room in the officer's quarters. It took some time to complete the surgery because of the need to treat combat casualties. In time, all of the cardiac patients were successfully treated and Murphy returned to his Air Force hospital in Cam Ran Bay.

I was a junior member of the cardiac surgery team, alternating between the jobs of second assisting and operating the heart-lung machine. I had a good opportunity to observe Murphy working in the O.R. Captain Snyder and Commander Larry Glass were the two cardiac surgeons on the USS Repose.

Both were knowledgeable and excellent technicians. Murphy shared the surgery with these two men and appeared in every way to match their skills.

While he was with us, I heard Murphy's story. He had been in the seventh year of a seven-year surgical training program at a prestigious medical center when he was drafted into the Air Force Medical Corps. He argued that he should be allowed to finish his last year of resident training, but the Air Force wanted him in Vietnam NOW! Somehow a compromise was reached where he came to Vietnam but was not required to wear a uniform. His regular outfit was polo shirt, Bermuda shorts, and sneakers. He wore the same outfit at his Air Force base. If there was a base inspection, Murphy was told to hide from the inspection team.

Murphy did not help with the care of the military casualties that were the biggest part of our work. When not doing cardiac surgery, he fished off the stern of the ship, using shrimp from the kitchen as bait. If a helicopter was landing, Murphy had to move off of the flight deck.

Murphy came to visit two more times, each time bringing more cardiac patients and two suitcases: one for his clothing and one for his liquor supply. He hosted an occasional cocktail party in his room. Liquor was forbidden on Navy ships, but a discreet violation of this rule may be tolerated. Our host told us of the saga of the Cam Ran Bay X-ray machine. The machine was late in arriving in country. When a large crate with the proper serial number did arrive, it was found to contain a 105 mm howitzer. The hospital was trying to trade the gun for a Jeep. Later, Army troops found the X-ray unit in a VC hospital...and blew it up.

Murphy was angry about being drafted and being sent to Vietnam. He retaliated in his own way by ignoring the military dress and regulations. As far as I knew, he seemed to be getting away with it. I found Murphy to be an amusing distraction, but, if every draftee followed Murphy's example, the military couldn't function.

TRIAGE

riage is the process of evaluating mass casualties, sorting them out and deciding on the priorities of treatment. Most physicians have never participated in triage. On the USS Repose, we had triage almost every day. It would be hard for civilians to imagine what it was like.

Triage took place on the stern of the ship. There was our flight deck, barely large enough for a helicopter to land, but land they did. A ramp led down from the flight deck to the main deck. The area where triage took place was in a relatively small compartment at the bottom of the ramp. Unlike most Navy ships, our vessel was painted white with large red crosses on the port and starboard sides. The masts were black to give better visibility for the pilots, who had to come down in all types of weather. The ships interior was Navy-grey. The bulkheads, deck, and overhead were all metal.

The triage area was crowded with a large number of personnel. There was a fireman in a heavy, reflective, fireproof suit on the edge of the flight deck, looking like the Michelin Man. A line of sailors stood by the ramp, waiting to transport the litters from the choppers to the triage room. A Marine gunnery sergeant stood to the side, straight and tall, silent and motionless. The sergeant must have been in his fifties, but he looked as fit as any Marine. He watched everything quietly but would spring into action if any armaments risked injury to the personnel. Eager doctors, in scrub suits waited to work on the injured, as soon as they were placed on the gurneys by the litter-bearers. Captain Snyder stood by the inner doorway, watching everything, and assigning his staff where they could be most effective.

The sounds of triage could be divided into three phases. First came the messages over the PA system. "Flight quarters, fight quarters. All hands, man your triage stations. Litter-bears, litter-bears, lay up to the flight deck, on the double!" Then, "All hands, stand by to receive twenty emergency medivacs." This meant we were receiving twenty wounded United States Marines.

You could not hear that message and not be affected. It was tense and exciting. When the litter-bearers began to file into triage with their stretchers carrying wounded troops, it was hard to breathe.

The second set of sounds were created by helicopters landing, and after discharging their cargo of carnage, taking off and making room on the deck for the next chopper. For years after, the distinctive sound of a landing helicopter made my hair stand on end. A helicopter landing meant trouble was coming. The musical "Miss Saigon" opened with the sound of a Huey landing. I experienced the same feeling in the theater as I had in Vietnam. I was with two other veterans, both physicians, when this occurred, and we all looked at one another wondering if we all felt the same thing. We did.

The third set of sound occurred when the Marines were being evaluated. That sound was eerie silence. It was strange to be surrounded by men with horrible injuries and hear no screaming or moaning. All you could hear was quiet and polite conversations between doctor and patient, but no complaining, only "yes, sir," or "no, sir." The stoicism of the wounded was profoundly moving to a doctor used to patients in New York City emergency rooms.

There was an urgency about the work that distracted from noticing things like temperature or comfort level. I was a physician seeing wounds more horrible than any I had seen before, but it was my duty to do my part to save the lives and restore the health of these American heroes. What I worried about was missing something or that we would not be able to treat one of them in time to save him. I did, from time to time, take a few photographs to show my doctor friends at home. Generally, they were too grossed-out by the gore to want to see more than a couple pictures. My job was to evaluate each case to see what the injuries entailed and to quickly present my findings to Captain Snyder who would be responsible for the determination of who needed surgery first and which doctors would be assigned to each Marine.

The experience of providing surgical care to our wounded troops was nerve-wracking and sometimes, exhausting. It was also exhilarating. It was a chance to make a difference in an otherwise horrible war. Looking back at my career, there are many things I'm proud of. I was fortunate to have been department chairman of hospitals at my medical school and I'd been president of my medical society. But what I'm most proud of is the work that I was honored to have been involved in with our troops in Vietnam.

IT'S A FLOATING WHOREHOUSE

As I entered the Officer's Club in Subic Bay, three officers from another Navy vessel were sitting at a table in the barroom. One of them, spotting the medical insignia on my uniform, jumped up in front of me and asked, "Are you on that hospital ship?" When I replied in the affirmative, he grabbed me and sat me down at his table. "What's it like being on a ship with women on board?" All three of the men were eager for my answer. I quickly wise-cracked, "It's a floating whorehouse." My answer had an effect like feeding steak to a starving man. The three of them ordered me a drink and began probing me for details. I didn't really have much to tell them this early in my tour. They were eager for any detail of life on a co-ed ship. At that time, in the fall of 1966, the USS Repose was the only vessel of the US Navy to have women on board.

Traditionally, women on a ship had been considered bad luck. Hospital ships had been the exception since nurses, a traditionally female occupation, performed essential hospital duties. Our ship had twenty-six nurses as part of the crew. We also had two ladies from the Red Cross and a female pharmacist. The other three hundred crew members were males. In truth, most of the nursing duties were performed by male corpsmen, working under the supervision of the nurses. The nurses were all professionals, having volunteered for duty on a hospital ship in a combat zone.

Needless to say, there was curiosity about our nursing staff in an area where "round-eyed" females were a rare commodity. Pilots landing in Da Nang would pass low over our ship and tip to one side to see if they could spot nurses sunbathing on the upper deck. Shore-based Marine officers would send invitations to the ladies to visit. One invitation from a helicopter squadron in

Chu Lai offered a softball game, barbeque, and initiation of a new "Pink Two-Holer." The Navy did have a rule that female officers had to be accompanied by male officers when going ashore. I was once one of the male officers chosen to escort our nurses to a party given by a Marine unit. The Marines focused on the ladies and flew them back to the USS Repose, leaving me to spend the night in Chu Lai. When we were in Subic Bay, senior officers would send their aides to the ship as soon as we docked to secure dinner dates with our female officers.

Was the USS Repose a floating whorehouse? The answer would be no. But it wasn't a convent either. Wherever men and women were working together in close proximity, over time romance could spring up. The circumstances of shipboard life did create difficulties in gaining the privacy necessary to consummate a love affair. There were also hundreds of peering eyes seeking to uncover if anything was going on. Time was also a problem. Most of the officers and crew were working long hours and were tired a good part of their time. However, where there was a will, there was a way. Senior officers had private staterooms in which they could entertain their female friends overnight. Rank had its privileges. My roommate had a lady friend who outranked him and had a stateroom to herself. He outranked me, but he preferred to spend his nights in her quarters, leaving me alone in the upper bunk.

Other romances were not always so obvious, but were suspected. There were couples that seemed to be together frequently, engaged in polite conversation, never exhibiting overt signs of overt physical affection. Did they have something going on between them? It was hard to know for certain. Once I saw a pretty, young nurse walking out of the treatment room used by our horny urologist. She had a wide smile on her face. The sign on the door read: "Urological procedure in progress. Do not enter!" It was natural to wonder what had gone on there.

The executive officer on the USS Repose was not a fan of having women on board his vessel. He did not want the USS Repose to be like a "cruise ship," and to guard against that possibility he made rounds on the USS Repose every evening with a flashlight, looking for evidence of mischief. One evening, he found what he feared was happening. He flashed his light on one of our lifeboats, slung out over the South China Sea, and he spotted two feet sticking out between the boat and its cover, one male and one female. He found his scandal. Officers on his ship were "doing it" in a lifeboat. The days of the "Old Navy" were over!

THE SEA

My involvement in the Vietnam conflict was to perform surgery on a hospital ship. I didn't feel that this involved danger to me. It did involve stress. The Marines fighting in the I-Corps area sustained high casualties on a daily basis and the doctors of the USS Repose were entrusted with saving their lives and restoring them to health. The ratio of combat casualties has been stable since the time of the Civil War; one-third of those injured die immediately. One-third had minor injuries that required minimal care. One-third had severe injuries, but could survive with medical attention. It was the latter group that provided our daily work. The USS Repose achieved the lowest death rate in the history of military medicine, less than one percent.

Many factors were responsible for our success, including rapid evacuation from the battlefield to the ship, improvement in medical care, and the very hard work of every member of the crew. We dealt every day with horrible, life-threatening wounds, often arriving in large numbers. I learned to dread the sound of helicopters landing and worried that we would not be able to get to all of the injuries in time. Somehow, that never happened.

There was a ready antidote for the stress and the gore, an old remedy that every sailor was familiar with. The eternal peacefulness of the sea was always close by. Our ship rarely docked. We were usually underway or anchored offshore. The soft sounds of the ocean had a soothing effect. The smell of the sea has a way of lifting a man's spirits. The vision of rolling waves could be entrancing.

One evening, Gerry Verdi and I had been doing surgery all night long and by the time we finished, it was morning and almost time for breakfast, to be followed by another day of surgery. Gerry grumbled that there wasn't time for sleep, what could we do? I suggested that we go out on the weather deck to get some fresh air. We stepped outside to be stunned by a sight that will always linger in my memory. The South China Sea was as calm as a lake. It was not yet light, but the sun was rising out of the ocean, like a huge, red ball, causing the sea to adapt the identical red hue. Then we witnessed, all around us, a small fleet of one-man fishing boats, heading directly out into the sea. Each boat carried a glowing lantern mounted on a pole on the stern. It was a scene that I would never forget.

The USS Repose crew had no days off, but there were moments of free time when it was possible to observe the events happening in the ocean. In the course of a year, I saw dolphins, flying fish, even a whale. In the evening, it was common to see sea-snakes up to six feet long gliding past our ship. Larry Glass had a powerful metal slingshot made for him. He used it to fire nuts and bolts at the snakes. He usually missed his target, but he attracted a large, cheering audience. People pay good money to engage in cruises. I got it all for free!

I know that the ocean is not always a friendly place, having experienced a typhoon. But the sea was my antidote for stress and fatigue. As much as I appreciated my year at sea, I was happy to get my feet back on dry land. After being discharged from the Navy, I was in no hurry to take another cruise.

NIGHT OF THE FROGMEN

I t was late spring in 1967 and the USS Repose was in Da Nang. When in that area, the USS Repose always anchored in the harbor about one mile from the airbase. It was a peculiar location because we were directly under the path for planes coming in for a landing. F4 phantoms on their landing approach would fly low, and as they passed over the ship and tipped to one side so that the pilots could get a quick look at the nurses sunbathing on the upper deck. The aircraft created a deafening amount of noise, but I suspect the nurses got a kick out of the attention.

On the afternoon of the strange occurrence, the USS Repose had received several Marines with shrapnel wounds from a mortar attack. I was involved in surgery to remove the shrapnel and debride the wounds. The surgery was routine, but it would run into the evening. As I was finishing my first case, a corpsman came into the room to pass the word that Marine intelligence had received information that the enemy was planning to sink our ship that evening and the ship would be sunk by under-water demolitions. The idea of Viet-Cong frogmen attacking my hospital ship seemed ridiculous. I really couldn't believe this information to be accurate.

Nevertheless, I was curious and headed up to the weather deck between surgeries to see what was going on. I found an odd scene on the deck. The first thing I saw was Ensign Hooper, the USS Repose paymaster, headed my way with a World War II rifle over his shoulder and a big smile on his face. Several of the junior officers were patrolling with rifles and scanning the waters of Da Nang Harbor for enemy attackers. I couldn't help but noticed that these line officers were glowing with pride and contentment in their new role as defenders of the USS Repose. They had signed on to become Navy fighting men, but were given the task of driving the hospital and medical staff to where ever they were needed. It must have been one of the most boring jobs in the Navy. Now they had weapons with live ammunition and the assignment to kill the enemy, if there was any. They approached their task with enthusiasm.

The sun was going down over the Da Nang hills. It was time for my next surgery and I headed back down to Operating Room #3, which was positioned against the port bulkhead and below the waterline. The surgery was underway when there was a loud *BOOM* and the bulkhead shook. This was followed, at intervals, by other booms from different areas. Larry Glass, without looking away from the surgical field, said, "They're dropping concussion grenades." We continued with the surgery as if nothing unusual was happening.

Word came to the team in O.R. #3 that the Seventh Fleet had ordered the USS Repose to leave Da Nang and proceed north to Dong Ha area. Before lifting anchor, the Captain requested a US Navy frogman team to inspect our hull to be sure that the enemy had not already affixed charges to the ship. It would be a bad thing for the ship to travel to Dong Ha and then be sunk! The inspection was completed very quickly. It was finished before I completed my operation. The USS Repose raised anchor and headed for safety at Dong Ha. I never got to see a frogman, friend or foe.

OPERATE IN YOUR UNDERWEAR

In late summer, 1966, the USS Repose was undergoing a replacement of its personnel. The original crew had boarded the ship in San Francisco, sailed to Vietnam, and had been operating in the Northern Provinces of the country, serving the Marine units in the region. As each of the crew members completed a year of service on board, they were rotated back to the states. Replacements were arriving almost daily. I was working in the surgery department and I heard rumors that we would soon be getting a new chief of surgery. The new man was said to have an outstanding reputation and he was the youngest captain in the Navy Medical Corps.

When the new head of surgery, Captain William Snyder, did arrive, I noted that he was not physically impressive. He wore thick, dark-rimmed glasses. He did not have an athletic build. He was clearly overweight which made him stand out because he was the only overweight doctor on the ship. All the physicians onboard were losing weight so rapidly that our pants were noticeably loose. If it weren't for the belts, our trousers would fall down. I mentioned to Rick Duboise that the captain would soon lose his excess weight. Rick disagreed and predicted that the new captain would stay heavy. (He was right.)

Our new leader was quiet in his first days on board. He was not performing any surgery. He was observing the work of his department, not making any changes immediately. He did make some suggestions regarding patient care, but nothing major.

We had another change of command in September. Chief of Nursing, Commander Kovcevich, a former Miss America contender, was replaced by Commander Hankey. The new nursing chief wasted no time in inspecting the entire hospital and initiating change. One of the first things she did was to ship all the scrub suits in the O.R. to San Francisco for repairs. The scrubs were probably left from World War II, or possibly the Korean War. They were old and riddled with holes.

The afternoon after the scrub suit send-off. A large group of casualties arrived onboard, all needing surgery. After triage, I was the first surgeon to get to the operating suite. As I entered the doctors dressing room, I was shocked to find that the shelves that were normally piled with scrubs were bare. Captain Snyder was the next to arrive.

I blurted to him, "There are no scrub suits. What should we do?"

The captain answered in a flash, "Operate in your underwear!" It was an order.

Within five minutes, six surgeons were at the scrub sink wearing only sneakers and boxer shorts. Entering the operating rooms, we donned sterile gowns, as usual.

For the next two and a half weeks, the routine of the underdressed surgeons continued. The repaired scrubs returned faster than I thought possible. There must have been a desperate plea for speed. I suspected that the captain had known about the shipping of our scrubs and had gone to the O.R. to be sure there was no delay in the emergency surgeries.

The episode greatly increased my appreciation of Captain Snyder. He was committed to fulfilling our mission of rapidly caring for the wounded Marines, despite all obstacles. We had a limited number of O.R.'s and personnel. As the director of triage, he made sure all the wounded were promptly and properly cared for, acting as the ringmaster of the surgical services. I was certain that his direction saved lives. He was the one to decide who should operate and who should rest to be ready for later surgeries.

"Walsh, sleep for four hours and the go to Room 3 to do two cases."

I did get to see the captain's surgical skills. He worked with Larry Glass on all our cardiac surgery cases. I assisted on many of them. He also helped me perform the intestinal repair on a young Vietnamese boy who had been shot in the rectum. It was a complicated and tedious surgery, and I was grateful for his guidance.

Captain Snyder was always serious when at work. He had to be. When it was time to relax, he could have fun like the rest of us. On one occasion, when the ship was in Olongapo for repairs, the surgeons took all the corpsmen on the surgical service out for dinner at a restaurant called Popaguio. The corpsmen ate and drank so much that we barely had enough cash to pay the bill. The corpsmen then invited the officers out for beers at their favorite club. Our surgery chairman was a big hit with the bar girls when he announced that he was "Captain Bonzo Stagg."

I will be forever grateful to the captain for his example and the help he extended me in furthering my surgical career. He did try to interest me in staying in the Navy, but he accepted my decision to return to civilian life. He granted my request to transfer to the orthopedic service to gain experience in the specialty I had chosen. He wrote an exceptional letter of recommendation for me. I still owed the Navy another year of service and requested a duty station in the Northeast to be close to the training programs I was applying for. I suspected that Captain Snyder may have had a hand in my being assigned to New London Naval Hospital and to the orthopedic department.

SEMPER FI

As a Navy doctor in Vietnam, I witnessed many situations where wounded Marines were retrieved from the battlefield and brought to the safety of our hospital ship. *Semper Fidelis* has been the motto of the United States Marine Corps for as long as anyone can recall. The term means "always faithful." It is often abbreviated to "Semper Fi." Marines take their motto seriously. No matter how difficult the situation, they will not leave another Marine behind.

There was one example of heroic rescue that was extraordinary. It had to do with a "Bouncing Betty." The name "Bouncing Betty" referred to a type of mine that, when triggered, "bounced" into the air and exploded with a deadly spray of shrapnel. The bouncing betty was a weapon manufactured in the United States and used by our armed forces.

During the Buddhist uprising, Arvin troops in Da Nang deserted, leaving 400 bouncing betties for the enemy to capture and use against our troops. In operation, the mine was triggered when a soldier steps on the buried pedal. When the foot pressure was removed, the mine would spring into the air and explode. In my year of treating wounded Marines, I never saw any survivors from the explosion of a Bouncing Betty. It was universally fatal.

One morning, the USS Repose had a call for Flight Quarters with only one helicopter landing and only one patient being off-loaded, this was unusual. The early morning was also an unusual time for a medivac flight. I reached the triage area before my colleagues and was waiting when the corpsmen loaded his stretcher onto the gurney where I stood. He became my patient at that moment. I began the routine of performing a history and physical exam with a series of questions to arrive at a diagnosis.

"What happened to you?"

He answered, "I got some shrapnel in my legs."

"What time were you hit?"

"Last night, about 1900."

I was surprised it had taken so long for him to reach our hospital ship. I asked what took so long for the medivac.

He replied, "There was a problem."

The young Marine then told me his story. He was one of several Marines wounded in a mortar attack. A medivac flight was called in. He was able to walk, but as he was making his way to the helicopter, he heard a "click" as he stepped on the path. He knew he had stepped on a mine. He froze and called for help. The lieutenant called for the engineers to come to deactivate the mine, a Bouncing Betty, but they would not be able to come until morning light. He would have to keep his foot on the mine for several hours. Although his wounds were not threatening, it was doubtful he could remain motionless on the mine until morning. His situation was grave.

Members of his squad gathered around their wounded comrade searching for a solution to his problem. Then one of his fellow Marines and another volunteered stayed with him until the engineers deactivated the mine. One Marine stood on his right, and the other on his left, through the dark hours. I couldn't imagine what they were thinking! If the foot slipped off the pedal, all three would certainly have died instantly.

In the morning, an engineer arrived to deactivate the Bouncing Betty and another chopper brought the wounded Marine to the USS Repose. His brave comrades did not accompany him on the medivac flight. I regretted that I never got to meet them. The surgery for his shrapnel wounds was routine, and our Marine was eventually able to return to his unit at Khe Sanh.

Many years have passed since this incident occurred. I have often thought about the bravery of these three Marines. Occasionally, I have told the story to a friend. The reaction has always been a brief introspective silence which I interpret as a self- reflection on whether they would have had the courage to stay with the wounded man. I was never sure if I could have done it.

VISITORS FROM THAILAND

The hospital ship, Repose, was in Vietnam to give medical support to the US Marines but we also provided care to members of other services from the US and our allies, including Arvin, Korean Marines and a few from Australia, New Zealand, and the Philipines. We had a number of civilian patients, mostly Vietnamese with war injuries or needing special care such as heart surgery.

One day unusual visitors arrived by military helicopter. An Asian man, a small boy, and a white male alighted and presented in triage. The white man wore a white shirt and black slacks. I couldn't say where he was from. He was vaguely European but, he spoke fluent English and Thai. I was told that he was a missionary and the other two were father and son. Increadably they had come from the far north of Thailand. The youngster had been found to have a heart malformation. The missionary had heard of an American hospital ship in Vietnam which was doing heart surgery, and suggested that they go there to have the heart problem corrected. To get to Vietnam the father and the missionary built a raft to float all three of them down the Mekong River to the Delta. Once in Vietnam, they hitch-hiked flights in military aircraft to the northern section of the country, finally taking a Marine chopper to the Repose.

The boy had the look common to sick children the world over. He was small and dusky and walked slowly with a stooped posture. His father was not a young man, but, he seemed vigorous and resolute.

The boy and his father were admitted to the International Ward while being evaluated for surgery. As a member of the cardiac surgery service it was my responsibility to see the boy each day on rounds. Due to the crowding on the ward the two of them occupied the lower bunk and two wounded Arvin marines shared the upper bunk. Their presence caused some consternation with the Vietnamese. None of them had seen Thai people and they were unable to communicate.

Our evaluation did reveal that the Thai boy did have a congenital heart condition which was amenable to surgical correction. Plans were made to go forward with his surgery. When there seemed to be a sufficient lull in combat operations, final preparations were made for the surgery. An operating room was prepared, sailors on the ship donated blood, as fresh blood is preferred for such major surgery. All was ready on the morning of the operation when there was a surprise. The boy's father suddenly announced that the surgery could not be done on that day. He had a dream on the previous night that this was a bad day for the surgery to be done. Our cardiac surgery team, the entire medical staff, and the entire ship's company were looking forward to the correction of the child's heart malformation. Despite our pleading, the father would not change his mind. Reluctantly the operation was cancelled and the equipment was removed from the OR.

Then came the next surprise. As soon as the room was shut down, came the call for Flight Quarters! We were receiving a large group of new casualties. We breathed a sigh of relief that one OR of the three that the Repose had was not tied up with heart surgery, impairing our ability to care for our new patients quickly. I had to shift gears quickly from the role of assisting at cardiac surgery to evaluating wounded marines for emergency care.

One week later the father had another dream that the next day would be a good day for surgery. The boy's procedure went forward without problems. Some people believe in the power of dreams. I never did but I may want to re-evaluate my skepticism.

BLOOD

The human body has about twelve pints of blood in circulation at any time. Blood is essential to life to deliver oxygen to the vital organs, the heart, kidneys, and the brain. We can lose a quantity of blood from trauma or disease and still survive if the bodies compensatory mechanisms are working. There is a limit. If too much blood is lost, the body is unable to compensate and vital functions will fail and death will ensue. Doctors treating trauma patients can prevent this catastrophic failure by giving the patient intravenous fluids, including blood transfusions, but there is a limit to how far we can go to prevent death in a severe trauma. Sometimes, it is not clear how far we can go.

All the doctors on the USS Repose could recall the day that Lieutenant Sperry arrived at Flight Quarters. One of the nastiest weapons devised for warfare was the Claymore Mine, a weapon designed to kill or severely wound its victim. Second Lieutenant John Sperry was unlucky to have sustained severe frontal blast from a Claymore. As the lieutenant was delivered to triage, it quickly became apparent that virtually every part of his body had been severely traumatized. He showed penetrating wounds of the head, neck, chest, abdomen, and the upper and lower extremities. Blood was freely pouring from every open wound. He exhibited signs of profound shock. He was unconscious and breathing with obvious difficulty. Some of the physicians in triage felt there was no chance of saving the man. Captain Snyder, Chief of Surgery, as usual made the decision and ordered blood transfusions and all efforts to save the Marine officer's life.

With blood transfusions running, the priorities for surgical repairs were established: stop the hemorrhage, restore the airway, repair the abdominal injuries, and address the other wounds. The plan meant that every surgical service on the USS Repose would be involved in saving this one life. I had never heard of this kind of effort before, but this was what had to be done. Just keeping up with the blood transfusions was difficult. Large cannulas were placed in the two un-injured extremities and pumps were used to force in bank blood as fast as it could flow. Before the first incision was made, a sixth unit of blood, half of the patient's volume, was flowing into him. He would require craniotomy, tracheotomy, thoracotomy, laparotomy, lower leg amputation, the removal of one eye and one testicle, as well as repair of wrist fracture. All the while surgery proceeded and hemorrhage continued. As more transfusions replaced the natural blood, clotting factors were affected, causing more bleeding.

On that evening, I was not in the O.R. as I was assigned to be medical officer of the deck, responsible for any in-hospital emergencies, and to respond to any helicopter landings.

Lieutenant J.G. Sheldon Green had just arrived in Da Nang Airbase on a chartered flight from California. He was exhausted but excited to be headed to his new duty, running the clinical laboratory on the USS Repose, Hospital Ship. He was proud to be a medical service officer with training in laboratory management. After presenting his orders, he was transported to NSA Da Nang and given a birth in the Officer's Quarters. He was told that he would be placed on the next helicopter flying out to the USS Repose. The hooch he was assigned to was the only unit without air conditioning. Despite his fatigue from the long flight, it was hard to get any sleep in the sweltering heat and humidity. At three a.m., the phone rang. A voice told him to get to the helicopter pad. A flight would be leaving for the USS Repose in a few minutes.

On the USS Repose, the surgeries on the lieutenant were proceeding, but bleeding remained heavy and a call was put in to Da Nang for more blood. A flight was promised with an immediate shipment of seventy-five units of blood for transfusion.

Sheldon climbed onto the UH-34. In addition to himself, the copter held the Marine pilot and seventy-five pints of whole blood. With minimal introduction, the UH-34 took off and headed northeast toward the hospital ship. A few minutes north of the base the copter passed over a group of mountains. At that point, a line of tracers could be seen heading toward the copter.

The pilot excitedly turned to Sheldon, saying, "Lieutenant, grab that machine gun and return fire."

Shelton paused briefly, thinking this could be a joke. Seeing the tracers heading toward him, he grabbed the 50-caliber and was somehow able to fire it, sending a stream of tracers in the other direction.

Flying north, the pilot turned back to Sheldon, saying, "Damn it! You missed them!" He turned the aircraft around for another pass.

At three-thirty a.m., I was awoken by a call informing me a copter was landing. Going to triage, I found that the cargo was a shipment of blood and one passenger. A young officer alighted from the aircraft soaked in perspiration, visibly shaking, and unable to speak clearly. I heard his tale the next day. With his transfusions, Lieutenant Sperry survived and made it back to his family in the states. Sheldon Green recovered from his introduction to Vietnam and went on to be a good laboratory administrator.

Three weeks after this episode, the medical staff of the USS Repose received a heart-warming letter from a Dr. John Sperry, M.D., Lt. Sperry's father. He reported that our patient was alive and slowly recovering at a VA Hospital. He went on to state that he knew, as a physician, how we might have been conflicted about whether to make the effort to save such a seriously injured patient, but that he was glad we did do what we did. It was rare to receive such a letter from family. Reading it brought relief and tears to a group of callused surgeons.

THE MISSING FOUR

I finished surgery early and had time to shower and change into my khaki uniform. I headed towards the Wardroom for the evening meal. There was time to step out onto the weather deck to take in some fresh air and to scan the view of the South China Sea and the beautiful coastline. In the Wardroom, seating was by rank, so my dinner companions were all lieutenants like me. The Filipino stewards always served a tasty meal. I was feeling relaxed and contented.

After dinner, I was planning to watch the movie in the Wardroom. I hoped that a peaceful night of sleep would follow. Just before the movie started, I received a message from Captain Snyder that the USS Repose would be receiving four prisoners of war, all needing surgery. So much for a restful night. I stayed in the Wardroom to see the beginning of the movie. I don't recall what was playing. Half the movies shown were worth watching. This must have been one of those worthwhile flicks, because I did stay until the end. I was surprised that the helicopter with the wounded prisoners hadn't arrived and I mentioned that to Captain Snyder, who promised to check on it. A message came back that the prisoners would not be arriving because "they all fell out of the helicopter."

I must confess that when I heard this news my first reaction was relief that I wouldn't have another night in the O.R. Then I realized that the prisoners had been thrown out of the helicopter. They had all been murdered! I was ashamed of myself for being happy to hear this news. What had apparently taken place on the helicopter seemed to me to be an atrocity. I was certain there would be an inquiry and punishment for the perpetrators. However, I never heard anything more about it. It seemed there would be no repercussions. But in the real world there were always repercussions. I thought about how the individual involved would be affected.

For myself, I did gain a few hours of sleep and was happy for that. There had been too many sleepless nights. I had no problem with treating enemy soldiers. The physicians code, since the time of Hippocrates, had taught that physicians must use their skills to help all in need of care. What I may have lost in the event was the experience and knowledge that I might have gained in the encounter. Every case was different and surgical experience was priceless.

For the four prisoners, the experience must have been terrifying. They had been wounded in battle and had been captured by their enemy and taken up in a Marine helicopter. Then the situation became a horror as they suddenly faced certain death being flung out of the craft and be smashed on the ground. Perhaps they stoically accepted their fate. That would be hard to imagine. Did they scream in terror or beg for mercy in a language that the enemy didn't understand? I suspected that was what had happened.

What was the story for the Marines who ejected their charges from the aircraft? What had they experienced in Vietnam that let them hate enough to murder their charges? And how did they feel about their actions later in life? Were they able to forget about their actions and live a normal life? Or did they experience feelings of remorse? Were they haunted by the memories of the screaming Vietnamese being flung into the air? Did they seek solace in drugs or alcohol, or perhaps suicide? There were always repercussions.

OOM-SHOOP

I received an order from Captain Snyder. He and Commander Larry Glass were asking me to follow up on a lead that they had received regarding an Arvin soldier who had received a gunshot wound to the chest causing development of a pulmonary artery aneurysm, a rare condition that they were interested in. They would like the soldier to be transferred to the USS Repose for heart surgery. They asked me to go to the Arvin hospital outside of Da Nang, find the soldier, and have him flown to our ship. They told me he had a prominent heart murmur that sounded like "*oom-shoop.*"

I accepted the assignment. It sounded like an adventure and I was curious to see more of the country than could be seen from the ship. We were anchored in Da Nang harbor. A motor-whaleboat was provided to transport me and my stethoscope into town. It was a beautiful, sunny day and the boat ride was refreshing. Landing at White-Elephant peer, I crossed the street to the White Elephant, Naval Headquarters where I was able to arrange for transportation to the hospital for wounded South Vietnamese troops. It was a short trip out of town. So far, so good.

Entering the administration building of the Arvin hospital, I announced myself at the front desk. I was surprised that no person there seemed to understand any English. My Vietnamese was very limited, but I did know the word for *doctor*, and I told the clerk I was "Bac Si Walsh." The clerk stepped out and soon returned with two very young Vietnamese physicians. Neither spoke any English, but they were friendly and tried to help. As I spoke, there was a lot of nodding and smiling. Finally, I said, "Ooom-shoop." Their faces lit up with recognition.

The two physicians let me out into the hospital, a sprawling facility spreading down the sloping hillside for a considerable distance. It was typical French Colonial style with multiple stucco buildings connected by covered walkways. It could have held several hundred patients. I suspected that my two companions might have been the entire medical staff for the large hospital. I was led into the first building and to the bedside of a young man who seemed to be cheerful and in good health. After an introduction, I placed my stethoscope on his chest and clearly heard *oom-shoop*! This was the man I was looking for! I tried again to communicate my desire to have him transported to the USS Repose by helicopter. More nods and smiles, no understanding.

On leaving the building, I realized that I had made no provision to get transportation back to Da Nang. I was reduced to hitchhiking, which I recognized could be a problem, an unarmed officer in the countryside. I was used to the relative safety of our ship and uncomfortable with travel in the countryside. Vietnamese riding by gave me a thumbs-up hand signal, which seemed friendly, but it could have been, for all I knew, an obscene gesture. I spotted a Vietnamese cyclist, heading towards me, balancing a package on the handlebars. Fearing that the package might contain an explosive, I ducked behind a tree. The man, seeing my fear, laughed so hard that he nearly fell off of his bicycle. Finally, I did get a ride from some Marines and returned to the ship. The wounded Arvin never did get transferred. The heart surgery team was busy and seemed to lose interest in the case.

I sometimes wonder about our man with the murmur. Did his aneurysm enlarge and burst, killing him? Or did he recover and go back to combat? Or is there somewhere in the rice paddies of Quang Tri a seventy-year-old farmer with *oom-shoop* in his chest?

GOTCHA!

How far would a lady go to please her man? How much could she put up with before she rebelled?

Connie Hurley was proud of her achievements in her profession. Ever since she was in grammar school, she wanted to be a nurse. She was attracted by the uniforms and the concept of helping people through the difficulties of illness and injury. She never wavered in the pursuit of her goal. Connie graduated first in her class from the nursing program at the University of Miami and then went to work in the operating room of Jackson Memorial Hospital. After one year of work there, she enrolled in a program for nurse anesthetists. She again graduated at the top of her class. She was immediately hired by Jackson Memorial and joined the anesthesia department there. The work was busy and exiting. In major surgeries, she worked under one of the anesthesia doctors, but in routine cases, she could administer anesthesia on her own. She loved the pharmacology involved and the independence. Her pay was enough for her to have a nice apartment and a new car.

Jackson Memorial Hospital was a major teaching hospital for the University of Miami Medical School. Students and residents rotated through the various departments. She enjoyed the enthusiasm of these future doctors, and she also liked the social life they brought to the scene. Connie was slender and attractive and her good looks did not go unnoticed. She easily brushed off flirtations from the older attending physicians, but she was open to the occasional fling with members of the resident staff. As the anesthetist for many surgeries, she was able to observe the surgeons work, and she favored doctors with the skill and maturity to make the hard cases look easy.

Harold Gable was a chief resident in neurosurgery. He was a tall, good-looking Southerner with an athlete's body and an unflappable demeanor. Connie did know he was married, but he had a reputation as a skirt-chaser. He had made a few conquests among the O.R. nurses. Connie was interested enough to request more work in the neurosurgery operating room. It didn't take long before Harold and Connie were exchanging glances over their surgical masks.

One evening, after they both worked on a long craniotomy, Harold surprised Connie by asking her if she would come to his on-call room. She surprised herself by quickly agreeing to join him. The two of them quickly undressed and threw themselves at each other. The sex was great for both of them; the best either had ever experienced.

Nights on the narrow bed in Harold's room became a frequent experience. Sometimes there were mid-day or morning liaisons as well. It was a basic sexual affair. Harold had a wife and daughter living near the hospital, and they avoided dating outside of Jackson Memorial. It was a nice fling, but it was obviously not going anywhere. Chief residents were in their last year of training in the hospital, and Connie knew Harold would graduate at the end of June and go on to practice neurosurgery somewhere else. She would miss him, but life would go on.

Where Harold was planning to go after his graduation was the Navy. He had made a commitment to serve for two years after finishing residency. The Navy spent little time showing Harold the basics of military life, giving him the rank of lieutenant commander, and sending him to Vietnam. He was the only neurosurgeon assigned to the busy NSA Hospital in Da Nang. Harold thrived in the busy surgical schedule. He was performing two major surgeries each day, more than any of his teachers in Miami. His rank got him a private, air-conditioned room. The food was okay and the medical staff was great to work with. There was the occasional party at the Stone Elephant Officers' Club. Despite the happiness he felt, he was missing something. He thought increasingly about Connie and the sex they had back in Miami.

Harold was a man of action and did some investigating to see if he could get Connie to come to Da Nang. There was a US Aid Mission Hospital across town, and they would be happy to have another anesthetist on their staff.

Connie was surprised to receive a letter from her former lover, even more surprised to receive his proposal for her to join him in Vietnam. Still, it could be interesting. She hadn't travelled much and this would be a chance to visit an exotic part of the world and to do some exiting work. She wrote back, accepting his proposal.

Connie was an asset to the USAID hospital which was overwhelmed with Vietnamese civilian patients needing surgery. She fell in love with the patients and grew to like life in Da Nang. Harold bought her a sturdy bicycle so she could come across town to spend her nights with him. The sex was still great. They were comfortable going out together with no Mrs. Gable within nine thousand miles of them. Their strange situation seemed to be working for them. She was becoming very comfortable with Harold, maybe falling in love with him.

Connie became aware that military personnel in Vietnam were entitled to a one-week vacation after six months in country. Harold hadn't spoken to her about the subject, but she supposed he was planning to surprise her. Once she saw a flier about Hawaii on his dresser, she began to get excited about a trip to the islands. Still, he mentioned nothing about his R&R.

The shock came on a Friday evening when they were sharing their narrow bed. Harold suddenly told Connie he would be away for a week. He was meeting his wife in Hawaii for a vacation, but it would only be one week, and they would be back together again. Connie exploded with rage. How could he do this to her after she had followed him halfway around the world? Harold tried to calm her rage to no avail. Connie bolted out the door, grabbed her bicycle, and pedaled furiously back to her quarters.

All day Saturday, Connie was too furious to do anything but sulk. How could Harold leave her behind and take his wife to Hawaii? She was the woman who deserved the trip after the sacrifices she had made for him! She was the woman scorned and he would reap her fury. On Sunday, she worked out her plan for revenge.

On Monday, she obtained what she would need from the hospital pharmacy and made all the arrangements she would need completed. On Tuesday, she set out on a quest to have sex with every Marine in Da Nang.

She focused on the men who were returning from areas where prostitutes plied their trade. By Friday, she was confident that she had gotten what she wanted.

On Saturday evening, Connie got a phone call from Harold. His plane had just landed and he was anxious to see her. She replied sweetly that she would be right over and wasted no time heading to his place. As she predicted,

Harold wanted immediate sex and she gladly gave it to him. Then, she politely excused herself and returned to her quarters. As soon as she was in her room, she used the first syringe to inject herself with the penicillin that she had secured. She already had a drip in her panties. She had the signs of coming down with Da Nang gonorrhea. She was certain that Harrold would soon have a nasty case himself. That would be his farewell present from her.

In the morning, she would be boarding the flight to Taipei, the first leg of her trip back to Miami.

YOU CAN'T ANSWER THAT, SIR

It was to be expected that communication by mail to and from a ship in Vietnam would be erratic and slow. It wasn't just the distance, but the fact that the USS Repose didn't remain in any one place or on any regular schedule. Sometimes the mail arrived by sea, during underway replenishment, and sometime it would arrive at some location on the land of Vietnam. The only combat fatality that the USS Repose suffered was the medical service officer who was killed in a mortar attack while getting a shipment of mail in Da Nang.

Despite the difficulties, mail did get to us and to friends and families back home. Mail call always brought pleasant excitement to all on board. There were usually delays, sometimes comically long delays, in receiving our letters. I got a letter inviting me to come for a job interview on March 1st. The letter arrived on April 15th. I couldn't have left my duties to go anyway. The few magazines we got were also outdated by the time they arrived. The only magazines the USS Repose received were *Jet* and *Ebony*. I read both whenever I could.

I wrote to my wife, my parents, and a few friends. I wrote to my brother who was fighting in the Central Highlands. We both tried to convince each other to be the one to go home, since two brothers were not supposed to be in-country at the same time.

I know that my letters home painted a rosier picture of things than was the case. I didn't want my wife, Nancy, to worry about me. Instead, she got the impression that Vietnam was a fun place to be. She complained I was having a great time in Vietnam while she was stuck in San Francisco. At some point, we started exchanging audio cassettes. That was how I heard the first sounds of our new daughter, who was born while I was overseas. Before going to sleep, I would play, over and over, her little sounds.

The USS Repose did possess a form of communication which afforded the ability to speak with family back home. It was referred to as "Phone Patch." Our radioman was able to contact a Ham Radio operator in California who could tap into the phone system and make calls to Nancy possible. This seemed incredible, but there were limitations. The entire ship's company had to share the radio. The service was only available at certain hours. The obstacle for me at times was finishing surgery by 1:30 a.m. After that time, calls could not be placed. All calls were censored.

My wife and I had planned to meet at Christmas time. Our ship had orders to visit Bangkok for a week. Nancy and a few of the other wives were planning to fly over to meet the ship there. A few days before we were to leave, we were told that plans had changed and we would be visiting Hong Kong instead of Bangkok. I panicked that we would be going to different places. I knew that I would have to use the phone patch option to get things corrected. I was able to make the call home. I told my wife that plans had changed and I would not be going to the place that I had told her we would.

After the "over," she asked, "Where are you going?"

I was then reminded that the calls were censored when another voice interjected, "You can't answer that, sir."

Fortunately, I had gotten my wife's trip itinerary and was able to answer, "On December 26th I'll be in the place you were going to be on December 24th." I hoped that she understood the meaning of my instruction.

Nervously, I disembarked from the USS Repose in Hong Kong harbor on December 26th and took a cab to the Mandarin Hotel where Nancy had planned to stay in Hong Kong. I could see from the cab ride that Hong Kong was an interesting city. The central area was affluent. The people on the streets were overwhelmingly Asian. Pulling up in front of the Mandarin, I could see that it was an elegant establishment. I walked across the glittering lobby to the front desk and asked the Chinese clerk if a Mrs. Walsh had checked in. He replied with a British accent that Mrs. Walsh was in room 807 and that she was expecting me. I made straight for the elevator, exited at 8, and knocked on the door of 807. My pregnant wife cautiously opened the door and, without a word, took me in her arms. I breathed a huge sigh of relief.

HONG KONG HOLIDAYS

In December, 1966, the military announced that a "Christmas Truce" had been negotiated. There would (theoretically) be no hostilities initiated by either side between Christmas and New Year's Day. As a consequence, the USS Repose would be allowed to leave Vietnam for the holiday. After some bargaining, it was finally decided that the USS Repose would go to Hong Kong for a week. The crew was excited to be getting a needed rest in an exciting port. My wife, Nancy, and a few of the other wives planned to meet the ship in Hong Kong. I was very excited.

The surgeons worked to complete all of our pending surgery cases before leaving Vietnam, but we ended up operating on some while the ship was underway. Father Coughlin celebrated Christmas mass on the ship and Lt. Commander Vest led a service for the Protestant crewmembers. We did have enough free time for a sumptuous Christmas dinner, including goose and apple pie. It was served while the ship was off the coast of Communist China. It was a great meal, the only goose dinner that I ever had.

On the morning of December 26th, the USS Repose sailed into Hong Kong Harbor. The city and the harbor were a beautiful sight. Victoria Peak rose up above a wall of modern sky-scrapers. The harbor was bustling with all kinds of traffic, ferries, junks, and ocean-going vessels. We anchored in the harbor and would use water taxis to go ashore.

I left the USS Repose, wearing a civilian suit and met Nancy at the luxurious Mandarin Hotel. I was feeling rich just being there. Our room was luxurious. The most peculiar thing was that it had a butler, a little Chinese man who sat outside the door ready to answer our every need. We didn't need much, but he would occasionally enter the room to do things like shine shoes or re-arrange things. I appreciated his industry, but the incursions into our bedroom were often ill-timed. Despite being pregnant, my wife looked great to me.

We spent the first day catching up. Then we started some serious shop-ping. Hong Kong had everything on sale and the U.S. dollar had great value in those days. The first stop was the clothier Loa Hy Shing where I was meas-ured for two new suits; one a Navy uniform and the other a sharp grey business suit. Everyone was having suits made. The lower priced tailors set up chairs on the sidewalks and stopped passing sailors, offering free beer. While the men sat and drank their beer, an assistant would be measuring them for a suit. The free beer kept coming while a suit was being constructed on them. Eventually, they would be presented with a passable garment and charged $35. These suits did have their faults. If the sailor raised his arms too abruptly the sleeves might come off.

The USS Repose had a ship's store and all of the store's profits went to the recreation fund for the crew. The store sold to the crew, our patients, and any of the many visitors to the ship. Merchandise for sale included Ja-panese cameras, stereos, and other expensive items. The profits diverted to the fund were enormous and would be used to throw a spectacular party for the USS Repose crew and guests. Over $10,000 was spent to rent the main ballroom of the Hong Kong Hilton for an evening of fabulous food and dancing. Young ladies from far and wide were invited to add to the enjoy-ment of the event. As it happened, a large group of fun-loving, single Aus-tralian ladies happened to be staying in the Hilton and they brightened the spirits of our lonely crew. I was content to be with my wife, but our bachelors also found happiness that evening.

There was a lot to see and do in Hong Kong. Nancy and I did the usual tourist things: Tiger Balm Gardens, the Victoria Peak Tram, The Harbor Tour, and the Floating Restaurant. We visited the New Territories and peered over the fence to view The Peoples Republic of China. We attended Sunday Mass in the Catholic Cathedral. The priest and the reader were both Chinese men with upper-class British accents. Wherever we went, we were clearly mi-norities in a sea of Chinese. It felt like an exotic tour for both of us.

I didn't have any work to do while the USS Repose was in port. My part-ners covered for me so that Nancy and I could enjoy our time together. I did take my wife to see the USS Repose, anchored out in the harbor. We took a water taxi and boarded the USS Repose. I was excited to show her my upper bunk in my little stateroom. We toured the wardroom, the helicopter pad, triage, and the surgical area. We visited my main ward, the "Tiger Service." There were some of the crew on board to greet us. Nancy commented that the USS Repose nurses we met were not as homely as I had described them in my letters.

The week was winding down and I would have to go back to my part of the war soon. I picked up my new suits from the tailor. They fit perfectly and were well-made. The sleeves would not come off if I raised my arms. Before leaving Hong Kong, there was one more treat to experience, New Year's Eve in this exotic city. It was an exciting time with banquets, bands, champagne and fireworks. I have never experienced anything like it anywhere else. For a brief time we all forgot about Vietnam and the war. But all good things do come to an end.

THE GOOD SHIP LOLLIPOP

Any person joining the military is given the advice "Don't volunteer for anything." I certainly didn't follow that advice as I volunteered to join the Navy and then volunteered for service in Vietnam. I wasn't as crazy as you might think. I joined the Navy because my draft status was such that I couldn't secure a position in a good surgical residency program without completing my military obligation. I chose the Navy as it offered better service situations than the other military branches.

After signing up, I enquired where I might be stationed. The recruiter offered one word, "Vietnam," but suggested I go to Washington to see what opportunities might be available. I took the train to the capital and met with a Navy officer, not much older than myself, and explained my situation and asked where I might serve. After a pause, he gave me three choices. I could ask to serve with a Marine unit in Vietnam, or request duty on a hospital ship, or seek assignment on an aircraft carrier in the Mediterranean.

I said, "Tell me about the aircraft carrier."

He laughed and said, "There's no such job. If you ask for that, you go to the Marines in Vietnam."

I told him I would be happy to serve on the hospital ship That is how I ended up volunteering for Vietnam.

It turned out that duty on the hospital ship was the best choice I could have made. The ship was comfortable and relatively safe and the work was exciting. I got to serve with an excellent medical staff and to do more surgery than I would in the best surgical training programs. The USS Repose was an old, World War

II ship, but the hospital on board could provide first-rate care. Most of my fellow physicians were career Navy. I had landed a good duty station.

After a few months on the USS Repose, the younger medical officers were asked to attend a meeting in the Wardroom. Captain Snyder was there to tell us that the shore-based physicians thought we had it too good and that they were being overworked. I doubted that anyone could work harder than we had been working, but the Navy decided that there should be a two-week doctor swap between the USS Repose and the Navy hospital in Da Nang. He was asking for two volunteers to go to Da Nang. None of us responded, and he went one by one asking for a taker without success.

Finally, Dr. Snyder asked if I would go to Da Nang. I responded that I would. Then, the other four physicians, almost in unison, asked why I had volunteered. I replied that I wasn't afraid of Da Nang. I had been to Da Nang. The next exchange might be to Con Thien. The doctor in Con Thien had just medivacked himself with the (correct) diagnosis of combat fatigue. None of us wanted to be sent to Con Thien. The others then changed their *no* to *yes* and Captain Snyder had to draw lots to choose the two to go.

After drawing lots, the two chosen to go to Da Nang were Jerry Verdi, my partner on the Tiger Service, and Royce Hansen my roommate. Jerry, a graduate of both dental school and medical school, had completed three years of surgical training and was preparing for a high-paying career in cosmetic surgery. Royce grew up in rural Idaho, married young, and had a family. Like many young interns, he developed a taste for hard liquor and fast women. This was not a good thing for a Mormon with a wife and four kids. Royce had to make some changes in his life. He was expelled from the Mormons and his wife, Joy, was content to be a long-term alimony recipient. Royce was the most popular doctor with our nurses. He outranked me and was thus entitled to the lower bunk in our stateroom, but he spent most of his nights in the nurse's quarters. He was a capable doctor and fun to be around.

In exchange for Gerry and Royce, the USS Repose would welcome two replacements for two weeks. My new roommate would be Lt. Hughie Hughes. The only thing I knew about him was that he had been involved in a famous incident in the Stone Elephant, the Da Nang Officers Club. At the entrance to the club was a sign saying, "Check All Weapons, Empty Bullets in Barrel."

Hughie caused quite a scare in the barroom when he aimed his forty-five at the barrel and fired his entire magazine into it. Reports said that my new surgical teammate, Dick Virgilio, was a good surgeon and a hard worker. He was known as "The Bear."

The exchange went well. It quickly became apparent that the workload was hard in both hospitals. I rarely saw Hughie awake. He kept to himself and never caused any trouble. It was a pleasure to work with The Bear. After two weeks, our visiting doctors returned to NSA (Naval Support Activity) Da Nang.

When Royce and Gerry returned from their temporary duty everyone wanted to hear about their experience. We had an impromptu meeting in the wardroom to get a report. Gerry Verdi started out by announcing, "We're losing the war." He was depressed by the number of amputations that he saw in Da Nang. NSA had a different case mix than he had seen on the USS Repose. We had more vascular and chest injuries but they had many more amputations. Royce didn't say much. He didn't give any comment on the nursing staff at NSA. I was curious about what their medical staff thought about our hospital out in the South China Sea. The crew of the USS Repose referred to our ship, AH-16 as Attack Hospital-16. Some of the crew called our vessel "The Pirate Ship" because our masts had been painted black to give better visibility to landing helicopters. Marines called us the "Angel of the Orient."

Royce laughed and replied, "They call us the 'Good Ship Lollipop'!"

CAO VAN NA

Of the thousands of patients that I've treated in my surgical carrier, most fade from memory after they have recovered and gone on with their lives. A few cases linger in my mind. One patient I will never forget is Cao Van Na. Cao came under my care while I was serving on the USS Repose in Vietnam in 1966.

Cao's story was especially tragic. Cao's father was serving in the Army of Vietnam, (Arvin). The Viet Cong came into his village in Quang Tri Provence to punish the family and to teach the village a lesson. They murdered Cao's mother in front of him, and then a Viet Cong soldier shoved a rifle into Cao's rectum and pulled the trigger. Somehow, the young boy survived the assault, but he had severe damage to his abdomen, especially to his lower intestines.

Before he came to the USS Repose, Cao was treated at another facility where he received a colostomy which diverted the intestinal contents away from his wounded bowel, saving his life. The result was that Cao was now a twelve-year-old boy who required a colostomy bag. Despite the trauma and the loss he suffered, the boy kept his composure. He never shed a tear or complained about his fate.

The plan for Cao was to repair the intestinal damage and, eventually, close the colostomy. This would require further surgeries and much time for healing. He, obviously, could not return to his village, so he remained on the USS Repose for several months. He was well enough to walk about the ship and smart enough to learn basic English. He was engaging and made friends of the Marines and the ship's crew. Everyone knew Cao's story and followed his progress. The Marines taught him to play poker, which he quickly mastered.

They didn't seem to mind when he walked away from the games with their money. He discovered the ship's PX and managed to have the crew and the Marines purchase items for him using his poker winnings. Somehow, he was able to sell his purchases on the Vietnam black market.

Cao was twelve years old, but he was the size of a seven-year-old. He was thin and wiry. Despite his condition, Cao never appeared sickly. He was high energy and all smiles. He had the high cheek-bones typical of his race. His small, dark eyes blazed with energy. He made friends with strangers quickly.

Like all the Vietnamese civilians, and some of the military, Cao was placed in the "International Ward," a small ward furnished with a few bunk beds. The ward was always heavily crowded. Designed to hold twelve patients, it usually had twice that number with two patients in the lower bunk and two in the upper. Often there were two soldiers in the upper bunk and two women or two children in the lower berth. The ward was run by Lt. Annelle Lee, a young lady of Chinese and Hawaiian background. Since Cao was the most fluent of all the Vietnamese in the English language, he was usually the intermediary between the patients and "Miss Lee." The Arvin Marines would follow Cao's orders. I thought of Cao as the mayor of the international ward.

Eventually, the time came for the reconstruction of Cao's rectal damage. I was directed to perform the complex repair, working with Captain Snyder, the Chief of Surgery. I performed the operation with Dr. Snyder directing all of my moves. It was a slow and careful reconstruction, requiring tedious removal of scar tissue and reorganizing the muscles of the rectal sphincter.

Cao made a quick recovery and was back on his feet and attending the evening movie for the patients and enlisted personnel. As he walked into the movie area, he was greeted by the sailors and Marines who wanted to know how the operation went. He responded by turning his back to the crowd, bending over, lifting his Johnny coat and displaying his new rear anatomy to one and all.

I don't know if Cao survived the war. I hope that he did. From time to time, I have tried to find Cao Van Na on the Internet without success. I have speculated whether he might have become a politician or a tycoon…or a prisoner of the Communist government.

DOCTOR PARK

Dr. Park was a small man, perhaps five feet, six inches in height. He was slender and wiry. He had a dark complexion and small, darting eyes. He was about ten years older than I was, about thirty-eight years of age, which qualified as old in Vietnam. He had dark brown hair, tinged with a bit of grey. His facial expression was always serious, consistent with the role he played in caring for the medical needs of a brigade of troops in combat. He wore dark green fatigues with no delineation of rank, and I never saw him with a weapon of any kind. He was the medical officer for a brigade of Korean troops in Vietnam. His Marines were all very fit and well-trained. They had an outstanding record in combat.

My surgical service, C-3, the "Tiger Service," was able to "kidnap" an English-speaking Korean corpsman who had come to us as a patient. His name was Park Sung Ju. He had been a veterinarian prior to entering the military and was proficient at minor surgery and wound car. We were well-equipped to care for Koreans, having a native speaker on our service. We usually had a census of four to five ROK marines. The Korean Marines were obsessive saluters. No matter how badly wounded they were, they insisted on standing at attention to give their open-handed salute to any officer walking by. I did every kind of gymnastic gesture to encourage wounded Koreans to lay still, rather than aggravate their injuries. They resisted, staggered to their feet, and gave me their best salute. The other strange thing about these troops was that no matter how fit and strong they were, they had no tolerance for narcotics and would nearly stop breathing after getting twenty-five milligrams of Demerol.

Every Wednesday, Dr. Park would visit us on the USS Repose to make medical rounds on his Marines. He visited each one, reviewed their charts and discussed their progress with Gerry and me. His English was not perfect, but we could understand each other well enough to collaborate on the care of our mutual patients. The Koreans were happy to see him and have a chance to speak with a doctor in their own language. It was a boost for their morale. Gerry and I would always invite Dr. Park to lunch in the wardroom. He rarely accepted the invitation because he was always seasick on our ship, no matter how calm the sea was. He endured the discomfort every week to visit and comfort his troops. He also arranged for transfers for Koreans ready to return to duty or needing medivac to Korea.

One Wednesday, our colleague did not visit the USS Repose. We missed him and speculated he was avoiding another day of nausea. We soon learned that the truth was different. Dr. Park had been killed by a sniper, shot between the eyes as he drove his Jeep to the helicopter base for his transportation to our ship. I was shocked to hear this news. He was a good doctor and a good man who died from an assailant he probably never saw. I would miss his weekly visits.

That was not the end of the story. The Korean Marines did not take the death of their doctor lightly. Their retaliation was brutal. They surrounded the village where the doctor died and lined up all the people in the town—men, women, and children—and killed them all. Then they killed every chicken, duck, and pig. They burned every house to the ground. Finally, they erected a large sign in Vietnamese, saying, "This is what happens to a village when a Korean is killed here."

During my time on the USS Repose, Dr. Park was not replaced.

NICK

My brother Nick was the fifth of the ten Walsh children. I was the oldest. Nick was quiet and well-behaved. He was also a puzzle. While his I.Q. tested at 148, "near genius" level, he remained a lackluster student. He narrowly graduated from college.

After college graduation, Nick did a year of post-graduate study at the University of Madrid. Our brother Jack did a similar year and graduated with honors. Nick had a different experience. He came home fluent in Spanish and speaking of his adventures, dating starlets, running with the bulls, and racing cars. His University of Madrid diploma was an obvious forgery. It was doubtful that he ever entered a classroom in Spain.

Shortly after returning home, Nick received a letter from Selective Service, informing him he had been selected by his fellow citizens to serve in the Armed Forces of the United States. He was sent to Oregon to train with the Army 4th Division. Nick accepted his fate. He reasoned that if he had to be a soldier, he would be the best soldier he could be. He excelled in basic training. He was chosen as the divisions best graduate and he received the rank of sergeant.

After training, Nick was sent to Vietnam with his division. This should not have occurred as it was stated military policy that two brothers would not serve in Vietnam at the same time, and I was already in country as a Navy surgeon.

My parents and siblings pleaded with Nick to request transfer. He politely, but stubbornly, refused. He was proud of his duty as a machine gunner on his APC. His unit was inflicting high casualties on the enemy. They were also sustaining high casualties. Nick and I exchanged letters. Despite my pleading, he still refused to leave Vietnam and suggested that I ask for a transfer instead. If

I went home and Nick was killed or wounded, I could never be comfortable with my family or myself.

In April of 1967, Nick wanted to visit me on my ship. He requested leave from his captain and was offered a pass if he would stage an ambush and bring the enemy bodies to the captain. He returned with ten enemy corpses and was given a four-day pass.

I didn't know that Nick would be coming for a visit. The morning of his arrival was anything but ordinary. At five a.m., an enemy rocket flew into a Marine bunker, injuring all six of the Marines inside. Three of the injured had traumatic eviscerations (intestines ripped out). All six were transferred to my hospital ship for surgery.

While six surgeries were taking place, the ship was refueling at sea. The USS Repose was on the port of the oiler and a destroyer was refueling on the starboard side. All three ships were heading north, doing fifteen knots.

All the surgeries were proceeding well when a message came over the PA system: "All hands stand by for collision!" This was followed by a loud CRUNCH and a frightening sound of ripping metal, followed by the ominous GONG, GONG, signaling general quarters. We had collided with the oiler. Most of the ships company knew that our sister ship, the Comfort, had a similar accident and sank in fourteen minutes!

However, the training and dedication of the crew prevailed. From the O.R., I heard "Damage Control Party to the forward section, starboard side, on the double!" Then, "Divers into the water!" The ship's divers jumped into the South China Sea to insert mattresses into the opening in the hull, saving the ship. We would have to sail to Subic Bay for repair in dry-dock. We were placed on diversion (no new patients).

Later that day, Nick arrived on the USS Repose by Marine helicopter. I was overwhelmed to see him. We wouldn't be leaving for repairs until relieved by the Sanctuary, the other hospital ship so we were able to have a couple days together. I was still unable to convince Nick to request a transfer. He bragged about his unit, as did I, and indicated he would stay the year in Vietnam.

When the time came for Nick to return to his unit, I was completely choked up. I held back the tears. I took a photo of him before he boarded the helicopter to start him on his journey back to his unit. I wanted the picture because I believed I would never see my brother again!

In time, I completed my tour of duty on the USS Repose and one day my replacement arrived. My new orders were to report to the US Navy Hospital in New London, my new duty station. I was delighted to be returning home to my wife and new daughter, born while I was overseas.

I left the USS Repose on a motor whale boat to Da Nang and a flight home. As the boat pulled away, I turned to look back at my ship vanishing in the distance. I was suddenly taken with a profound sense of sadness and guilt for leaving the USS Repose, my fellow surgeons, and our US Marine patients. I hadn't expected leaving to be so hard. I understood then why Nick couldn't bring himself to request transfer home.

WORMS, TIGERS, SHARKS, AND SNAKES

There were many ways to get injured in Vietnam. The most obvious was enemy fire. You could also be injured by accidents, including "short rounds." However, there were other perils to life in Vietnam.

Worms

Rick DuBoise grabbed my arm as I was leaving the wardroom, saying, "Let me show you something gross." Rick was a GMO (general medical officer) on the medical service. He was a good doctor and a good guy. His special interest was infectious diseases and he delighted in the variety of tropical-diseases in Vietnam. Rick led me to the medical ward and into the treatment room. Sitting on the counter was a bed pan, and in the pan was the thing that Rick was trying to gross me out with. Three large red worms, each two feet long wiggled in the pan. They were attracting a procession of curiosity seekers, including the Marine who had recently been carrying them in his intestine.

The most common animal attack I saw in Vietnam was roundworm infestation. The worms inhabited the victim's intestinal tract and could grow quite large. The larva entered the body through the skin, the respiratory tract, or the mouth. The larva migrated to the intestine and were nourished by the victim's diet. They may thus cause weight loss, intestinal bleeding, or abdominal cramps. They may be diagnosed by inspecting the stool for eggs from the worms. If the worms were large, they may be seen on X-ray.

The treatment of roundworms in Vietnam involved the oral administration of Paraldehyde followed by an enema. The Marines liked the Paraldehyde because it made them high. It must have had a similar effect on the worms, because the enema released the hold they had on the bowel, letting them all wash out. They were an awesome sight.

Tigers

One evening, I was finishing a surgery and became aware of some commotion in the staging area. Investigating, I heard that a Marine had been brought in after been attacked by a tiger. He had been on patrol in the jungle near Khe Sanh and felt something hit him in the back of his shoulder. Thinking that it was a prank by one of his buddies, he turned to face his comrade, but instead he came face to face with a Bengal Tiger that had taken a large bite out of the right shoulder. He was able to kill the tiger and was medivacked for repair of tiger bite. The Western Highlands of Quango Tri Province has had tigers for years. The local tribes build their houses on stilts as a protection from the wild cats. There were several tiger vs Marine confrontations during the war, with the Marine winning in every case. A few Marines had tiger pelts shipped home.

Sharks

On another day, I received another Marine with an unusual tale to tell. He was medivacked for wounds on his right leg from a shark bite. It must have been a small shark, or one that wasn't hungry, because the damage was not severe. He did require surgical repair, but not amputation. He told me his story. He was a Japanese-American from Hawaii and survived a year of combat in Vietnam without receiving a scratch. During the year, he fell in love with and married a Vietnamese girl and attempted to bring her back home to Hawaii. Her visa was held up by red tape, so he asked to remain in country to be with his wife. He was re-assigned to remain in Da Nang and was made a lifeguard on China Beach. There, while taking a morning swim, he suffered his first injury in Vietnam.

I cleaned and repaired his wounds and he was able to return to his spouse in Da Nang.

Snakes

On another day, the USS Repose was notified in advance of a patient, already in flight to the ship who was reported to have been bitten by a venomous snake. The heads up gave me a chance to research the best way to treat snake bite. I had never before had to treat one. We've all heard the common theory of lancing the bite and sucking out the venom. This theory qualifies as an "old wives' tale." Commander Glass, my superior officer, let me know that proper treatment for snake bite is administration of anti-venom. The Navy had available "Southeast Asia, multi-valent snake anti-toxin," good for four out of five poisonous snakes in the region. Only the sea snake had no antidote for its poison. Since our patient was bitten on land, I didn't worry about sea snake bite. Because the toxin causes severe muscle swelling, I had to be ready to do a surgical fasciotomy, loosening the muscle covering to relieve pressure in the muscle compartment.

My victim arrived promptly by helicopter, and he told me his story. He had been caught in an ambush and came under machinegun fire. He spotted a foxhole and dived in to escape from fire. He was shocked to find that he was sharing the foxhole with a small snake. Before he could kill the snake, he sustained a bite in his calf. He began to feel dizzy and ill and felt a tight, burning pain in his calf. He was rescued from his peril and flown to the USS Repose. I packed the swollen calf in ice gave the anti-toxin a and took him to the O.R. for a fasciotomy. He did well. I was glad not to have had to suck out any venom.

PURPLE HEART

P hysicians are supposed to be non-combatants and would not usually be recipients of the Purple Heart, the medal given to members of the Armed Forces who are wounded in battle. I did know two doctors in Vietnam who were nominated to receive the Purple Heart. The first was Dr. Alan Playford, an anesthesiologist from Alabama and a career Navy officer. Dr. Playford received a human bite on his hand from a prisoner of war that he was anesthetizing. A human bite could be a severe injury, but after he had the wound cleaned and received a shot of antibiotics, he was able to finish the case.

When Dr. Playford heard that he was nominated for the medal, he was angry, protesting in his Alabama drawl, "I will not except the medal! I do not want on my record that I was bitten by a patient!"

The second physician was a different story. Douglas Moffet was a flight surgeon for a Marine helicopter squadron in Chu Lai. Because the pilots under his care were rarely sick, they reasoned that Moffet was not a real doctor. The squadron was known as Klondike and they called their doctor the "Klondike Quack." One evening, the Klondike Quack was asleep in his bed when a mortar shell went through the roof of his hooch and imbedded itself in the floor, next to his bed. It did not explode. In a panic, the doctor ran out the door, tripped, and sustained bruises, and abrasions to his shin. The Marines thought that this was good enough for a Purple Heart and thus began the "Legend of the Klondike Quack."

Since the USS Repose was a hospital ship, we had many Purple Heart recipients on board. General Walt, the Marine commander in Vietnam, would come aboard once a week to distribute up to a hundred medals to the newly wounded. It was quite a production. The general brought a staff to assist in the enterprise. A junior officer would lead the general to each deserving Marine announcing his name, and producing a Purple Heart. The general said a few kind words to the recipient while pinning the medal on his pajamas. Another officer photographed this event and handed the Polaroid picture to the Marine. Then a sexily-dressed starlet would give the Marine a kiss, and this too would be photographed. After giving the necessary awards in each hospital ward the group moved on to the next ward to repeat the process.

After General Walt's party moved on, the Marines would erupt in excited conversation usually focusing on the kiss. It had been a long time since the last kiss for most of them. One of the young ladies gave each of the Marines a French kiss. That was a big hit!

TYPHOON NANCY

he USS Repose was in Subic Bay for a six-day visit and life was less hectic. I still had to look after the patients on the Tiger Service, but the census was reduced as we were not getting new admissions daily. Those patients who had recovered were discharged to their units. Patients who would not be able to return to combat were medevacked home. My rounds that morning were leisurely. There was time to chat with the Marines about their lives.

I headed for lunch in the wardroom, something rarely possible when we were in action doing surgery as O.R. scrubs were not allowed in the wardroom. The lunch was not crowded as many of the officers were relaxing at the recreational facilities on the base. The conversation at the table focused on two topics. The first surprise was that orders had changed and the USS Repose would be leaving Subic before nightfall. The second topic concerned Typhoon Nancy, a giant storm that was heading our way with winds of 120 miles per hour. All ships in the fleet had been ordered to take shelter. The medical staff was concerned about why we might have been ordered back to Vietnam, fearing that the marines might be sustaining heavy casualties. The line officers were concerned about being ordered out into the storm.

The crew and officers of the USS Repose were being rounded up for our departure, back to the war. All afternoon ships of every description could be seen heading into the harbor. I should have been more concerned about the looming danger that we were heading for. Without fanfare, the USS Repose raised anchor and set out to sea. Leaving the harbor, we passed the USS Forestall, our first super carrier and an impressive sight. The sun was shining and the sea was calm. There was no hint of what was ahead for the USS Repose.

That evening, the stewards served a dinner of chicken adobo. After dinner there was a movie in the wardroom, *Flying Leathernecks*, starring John Wayne. All the chairs were taken, so I sat on top of some cabinets in the back of the room.

Before the film ended, a message came over the PA, saying, "All hands prepare for heavy seas." With that, I was suddenly rocked off my perch on the cabinets as the ship was being tossed about by massive waves. Nancy had found us. Everything changed very suddenly.

Walking became difficult. Furniture was being thrown around. A good number of the crew began to experience sea sickness. I was happy not to have that problem. When I got back to my quarters, I found that siderails had been attached to my bunk. Since I had an upper bunk, this was welcomed. My room-mate Royce outranked me and had the lower bunk, although he preferred to sleep in the nurse's quarters.

For two days and two nights, the USS Repose was in the arms of Typhoon Nancy. The howl of the powerful wind was frightening and continuous. When waves crashed on the upper-decks, it felt like a collision. Sometimes the storm would lift the entire ship completely out of the water, causing a weird vibration due to the propeller spinning in the air. Most frightening was the creaking sounds that our old ship made when it's joints were stressed. I wondered if we would make or if I would die at sea. The ship was listing forty degrees to port and then hesitated as if it might keep going and the capsize. Then it would, slowly list to starboard, and repeat the process.

On day two of Nancy, only one of the four tables in the wardroom was occupied. Sea sickness had taken its toll. We were served a soup, and it was the only time in my life that I experienced waves in the soup bowl.

Despite the weather, I had to round on my patients who were all, thankfully, doing well. As I was leaving the ward, I ran into Captain Snyder, Chief of Surgery, who told me he needed me in the O.R. in ten minutes for an appendectomy. One of the nurses had developed an acute appendicitis and would need an emergency operation. Normally an appendectomy was a routine procedure, but operating under these conditions would be anything but routine. I was happy to be assisting the experienced Dr. Snyder. The ship was listing forty degrees in each direction and the operating room was as well. Our patient was strapped securely to the O.R. table. The O.R. staff could only brace ourselves. The team consisted of Captain Snyder and me, Roman Wandalowski, the anesthesiologist, and two O.R. techs, known as "Cowboy" and "Psycho."

The operating table was locked into place and wasn't a problem. The Mayo stand and instrument table were secured with sandbags in the hope that they wouldn't move. After uneventful prepping and draping, the incision was made and extended through the superficial layers. Our patient was slender, making the approach easier. As the deeper layers of fascia and muscle were divided, the abdomen was entered, and I placed the retractors to expose the appendix. At that moment, a particularly large wave rocked the ship, and the instrument table broke loose from the sandbag mooring and flew across the O.R. heading away from us. Then the list headed in the direction of the operation and the table came flying towards the surgeons, hitting the O.R. table with instruments, including knives and scissors hurtling through the air. Recovering from this excitement, we finished the operation uneventfully.

After two days, the ship did reach Dong Ha, but weather conditions made helicopter operations too hazardous and we were unable to admit any patients for two more days.

MYRNA

J eremy Plotski was much loved by his mother. Myrna Plotski married at age twenty-one and almost immediately began praying to God to send her a son she could treasure and nurture. She and her husband, Walter Plotski, were able to purchase a comfortable home in a respectable neighborhood in Newburgh, New York. The structure contained an extra bedroom, which they referred to as "his room." As time passed, they acquired furniture appropriate for a boy, preparing for his arrival.

Life in Newburgh, their adopted town was good for the Plotskis. Walter, a pharmacist, found plenty of work in his field. After a while, he was able to purchase his own pharmacy and he worked hard to make it successful. He was good at remembering the names and the needs of his customers. He was well-liked, and his business prospered. Myrna volunteered at the Jewish Center and could be counted on to make every event successful. Still, every night she continued to pray for the little boy that would make her life complete. Her friends and cousins were getting pregnant and bragging about their wonderful children, but Myra's prayers went unanswered. She and her husband sought out expensive consultants and they were assured that they were both healthy and capable of producing offspring. Still, nothing happened.

The Plotski family prospered. Walter was able to develop an investment program for the future. They joined a country club. They bought a larger, nicer home in the best part of town. It had a larger room for "him." Walter became an active member of the local Chamber of Commerce. Still, no pregnancy occurred. Walter suggested considering adoption but Myrna would not think of it.

Finally, as Myrna was approaching forty years of age, she became pregnant. She was certain that this was the son she had been waiting for. She gave thanks to God and increased her preparations for the birth of this miracle child. Having a baby at Myrna's age was no piece of cake, but she did everything possible to make it a perfect pregnancy. Everyone stated that no mother-to-be was ever more radiant than Myrna Plotski through her nine months. At last came the delivery. It was a son and he was named Jeremy.

Myrna was overcome with joy. Her life was consumed with caring for her son, her pride and joy. He had to have the best medical care, the best diet, the best infant attire, the best of everything. She bored her friends with her constant talk of her wonderful child, but they were all happy for her. As Jeremy grew, she began the ritual of serving him breakfast in bed. As he progressed from the toddler stage through boyhood and adolescence, the practice of breakfast in bed continued. It was Myrna's way of thanking Jeremy for his existence.

In high school, Jeremy was a good student. He was popular with his classmates but he was not an athlete. He was undecided about what to do with his life, but it was assumed that he would attend college. He began to follow stories of the war in Vietnam nervously. Like all American boys, he registered for the draft at age eighteen. Jeremy was not alarmed when he received instruction from the Selective Service Administration to report to the facility on Whitehall Street in Manhattan to undergo a physical examination for the purpose of classification. It sounded routine.

On the day of his appointment he took a bus to Manhattan and a subway to the Whitehall Street area. He walked into the large, aging, and somewhat decrepit government building which was filled with hundreds of young men of about his age. Jeremy followed direction and was led into a sort of locker-room where he was instructed to disrobe, leaving him and all the others in undershorts. The group was arranged in a long line abreast while various examiners performed the most perfunctory physical examination imaginable. One walked down the line with a stethoscope, listening to one heartbeat in each man. Another used a flashlight to peer into each mouth. Then there was the famous "Bend over and spread your cheeks." Each man was given a healthcare questionnaire to complete and turn in. They were allowed to dress and wait.

After a while, Jeremy was called into the doctor's office for a brief review of his file. The doctor said very little, but gave the impression that all was well. Jeremy resumed his place in the waiting room. After a while a list of names was read out. The list included Jeremy's name. The young men on the list were told to remain. Everyone else was dismissed. Something disturbing seemed to be happening. A medic addressed the small group, informing them that they had done so well on the exam that they would be assigned to the Marine Corps and a bus was waiting outside to take them to Paris Island for training. Total shock! Could this be possible? The Marine Corps was traditionally a volunteer outfit, but at times recruiting did not produce enough troops and the draft was needed.

Jeremy felt that he was riding through the night on a bus, heading toward his doom. How had this happened to him? He was unprepared and frightened. It was about to get worse. The bus lurched to a stop and all hell broke loose. Screaming crazy men pushed him off of the bus and into more chaos. He was issued uniforms, had his hair shaved off, and was assigned a bunk in a room full of strangers. There was no breakfast in bed. Worst of all, he was constantly harassed and by a tall, maniac with a shrill voice and a demonic temperament, Sergeant Bruce Pinkernell. Jeremy felt that this man was badly treating him. Was he anti-Semitic? Was he demented? What was happening?

The first chance he had, Jeremy wrote to Myrna, describing the horrors being inflicted on him by Sergeant Pinkernell. Myrna was horrified by the letter. What was being done to her precious boy? She sprang to action, notifying her congressman of her concern about improper treatment of her son. She arranged for an immediate trip to Paris Island to correct the mistakes the Marines were making with her boy. Armed with a letter from her congressman, the Honorable Hamilton Fish, she stormed onto the base and confronted the Commandant, demanding to speak with Sergeant Pinkernell. There was no stopping this enraged woman. The Sergeant was produced and Myrna immediately gave him an earful. The Sergeant, finally given a chance to speak tried to explain to Myrna that her son was being given training that would help him survive in combat. Myrna coolly told the Sergeant that she had raised her son properly and he would NEVER shoot anyone.

The Sergeant was unable to say another word. In his fifteen years as a Marine, he had learned a few things. One thing he knew well was push-ups, and push-ups would be his answer to the Plotski matter. Every time Jeremy encountered the Sergeant, he had to drop to the ground and execute endless push-ups.

Jeremy did survive the Marine Corps and a year in Vietnam, working at the Supply Depot in Dong Ha.

THE LITTLE BOY

Doctors can often recall a case that went very well. We can never forget a case that went badly.

From time to time, when work is not busy, and when my mind is not engaged with any particular - task, my thoughts might drift to memories of the little boy. I refer to him as "the little boy" because I never learned his name. I remember when he became my patient on a day, fifty years ago. He was brought to the USS Repose by a Marine Major, who was involved in dealing with collateral damage in the war.

The major told me that the boy had been living with his grandmother in a small house in Da Nang. That information would imply that his parents might have been killed, or perhaps, they might have been away fighting in the war, for one side or the other.

The major related that a Marine aircraft had accidently dropped a bomb on the house, destroying it. The boy was injured in the incident and was being brought to the USS Repose for care. He further stated that the grandmother was paid twenty-five dollars for the loss of here house and he insisted that twenty-five dollars was a fair price.

For some reason, the boy was placed under my care. He was not admitted to the international ward with the other Vietnamese patients. He was admitted to Ward C-3, the "Tiger Service," a sixty-three-bed ward which primarily treated wounded Marines. He was placed in a bed in the front of the ward, near the nurse's station and across the aisle from two US Marines.

Right after admission, I did a thorough exam on the boy. He appeared to be two or three years old. He was not in any major distress, but he was not responsive to any stimuli. His pulse, blood pressure, and respirations were all normal. His eyes were open, but they didn't seem to see anything. He stared at the overhead. Examining his body, I found no wounds. Using my stethoscope, I heard that his chest was clear, his heart sounds were normal, and his bowel sounds were regular. I ordered routine blood tests, urinalysis, and X-rays of the chest abdomen, head, and extremities. Encouraged by the boy's young age and the absence of abnormal findings, I expected he would soon snap out of his stupor and return to good health.

I checked on the boy that evening and he seemed to be unchanged. His vital signs remained in the normal range. I assumed he would be better in the morning. But the following morning was the same. The physical exam again showed no abnormalities. The laboratory tests and the X-rays all came back normal. He was breathing on his own and taking liquids by mouth. He showed no interest in his environment despite the effort of the nurses and the corpsmen and the Marine patients to engage him. I believed that he would snap out of his state quickly.

On day three, I went to see how the little boy was doing. He was still in the same position in his bed, but he was not breathing. He had died during the night. I never knew what had caused his death. Over the years, I have wondered what I had missed and what I might have done to save his life. In a modern medical setting today, the little boy would have had sophisticated medical tests. He would have CAT scans and MRIs. He would have been admitted to a pediatric ICU, and had the attention of a pediatric intensivist. The little boy had none of these things. He only had me, and I failed him.

LUCK

I rish joke: Murphy is the luckiest man alive. He was run over by an ambulance. The outtake is, even if you suffer a misfortune, the circumstances can make you "lucky."

I had a patient who was a crew chief on a Marine helicopter flying over the coast near Dong Ha, above the coast road known as the "Street Without Joy" during the French War. A single round of enemy fire penetrated the chopper and entered the Marine's chest. The helicopter pilot knew exactly what to do. From his altitude, he could see a white ship with red crosses on its side, anchored off the coast. He radioed ahead and the headed directly for the ship's flight deck. The wounded man was carried into the USS Repose and was soon in surgery, within minutes of being wounded.

People said, "What a lucky guy!"

Lt. Commander Vest was the Protestant chaplain on the USS Repose. He was proud to have a son serving on a swift boat patrolling the South China Sea in the same area of operation as the USS Repose. One day while patrolling, the younger vest was struck by enemy fire. He was taken to the USS Repose for treatment. He had sustained a gunshot wound to the spine, an injury with the potential for paraplegia. The bullet that had stuck the young ensign had been fired from an AK-47 assault rifle while the swift boat was three hundred meters from the shore. The AK-47 derived its destructive power from its high muzzled speed. This bullet left the rifle at full speed and quickly closed the distance to the swift boat. The humid Vietnamese air slowed it very little in its journey. It next encountered the bulkhead of the boat. Had the boat been manufactured of steel, it might have been stopped. But the swift boat was constructed of aluminum to give it greater speed.

The bullet continued on its journey, somewhat slowed. Next, the AK-47 round struck Ensign Vests Kevlar flak jacket with enough power to penetrate, piercing the shirt and tee shirt and then the skin, adipose tissue, and muscle above the spine. Finally, it smashed through the lamina, the boney roof of the spinal canal. There it stopped, out of energy and unable to penetrate the dura, the covering tissue of the spinal cord.

The surgeons removing the bullet found no nerve damage. The Ensign was lucky I had another Marine patient who had been shot in both arms and both legs. You might think that he was very unlucky, but not if you knew his story. This young man had been knocked flat on his back by a blast which had stunned him. He awoke to find a North Vietnamese soldier standing over him and aiming his rifle at him. Even worse, his own M-16 had jammed and would not fire. His situation was beyond desperate. The enemy soldier appeared not to be in a hurry. He aimed carefully and fired four shots, hitting him in each arm and each leg, then he turned and walked away. Our man's injuries were serious, but not life-threatening. What had happened? The enemy soldier could have easily killed the Marine, but instead chose to wound him in a way that would remove him from the conflict. I am awed by this merciful act by an enemy combatant. Our Marine was lucky.

AK-47

It was a desperate time. The surgeons on the USS Repose had been working day and night for too many days. We were exhausted and we were barely keeping up with the casualties that kept arriving, and they just kept coming.

The weapon giving us so much work was the AK-47 rifle, the primary arms used by the enemy. The AK-47 (Kalashnikov) is a very dependable weapon that has a high muzzle speed and good accuracy. The bullets used in the AK-47 in Vietnam were made in China and had copper jacket wrapped around a lead core. The bullet made a small entry hole on hitting its target, but the energy of impact created a large cavity in human tissue. The copper jacket shattered on impact and went off in different directions, causing even greater damage. These were the wounds our troops were suffering and were exhausting the surgical staff.

It was well after midnight when another wounded Marine arrived in triage. He had an entry wound in the flank, directly over the kidney and was thought to have a kidney injury. Jim McGowan, the urologist was assigned to take him to the O.R. for exploration and probable nephrectomy. Captain Snyder asked me to assist McGowan because "You're the most awake one I've got." I hadn't worked with our urologist before. He was something of a loner and was somehow different. He had been a rifleman in the Army before becoming a Navy doctor. He wore a sharp-shooter badge on his khakis, which was a very unusual thing for a doctor to wear. He spent a lot of time in his quarters and was rumored to have a private liquor supply, although I never smelled liquor on his breath or saw him inebriated.

We entered the O.R. at two a.m. The team consisted of McGowan, myself, Roman Wandelowsky, the anesthesiologist, and two tired looking techs. We were the only ones in the entire suite, besides our patient. It was deadly quiet. The ship was anchored and rolled very little.

After prepping and draping McGowan made a midline abdominal incision, rather than the flank incision I was expecting. This approach provided access to the rest of the abdomen. As the belly was opened, a large amount of fresh blood came into view. The kidney area was explored by positioning the retractors. There was no bleeding coming from that area and palpation revealed no kidney defect. Looking above the kidney, it was apparent that the spleen was damaged and bleeding profusely.

McGowan stood still and addressed me saying, "There's no kidney damage. It's your case."

A spleen injury should not have been my case. It should have been a case for the most senior surgeon available, especially if the wound was caused by an AK-47 round. It was obvious that McGowan did not want to take on this surgery and was happy to give it to me. I knew that this was the kind of surgery beyond what my training had prepared me for. It was a situation where bad things could happen fast. I quickly considered my options. I could have the corpsman wake up Captain Snyder or Commander Glass, but I was reluctant to do so because I knew they were exhausted, and it would take time for them to arrive in the operating room. With a hemorrhaging patient, time was important. I was already scrubbed in on the case and was ready to take it on. That was probably a cocky attitude in a young, partly trained surgeon, who had never done a splenectomy or seen one caused by an AK-47.

In truth, I didn't want to admit I was intimidated by the task. I grasped the suction device to clear the blood in the upper, outer quadrant and aimed the O.R. light into the area. There, I could see the spleen, blown apart and bleeding profusely from all quadrants. Two reflections from copper fragments caught my eye. I paused briefly, considered my options, and then asked for a hemostat and used it to clamp the splenic artery, the first step in removing a damaged spleen.

FORRESTAL

The USS Forrestal and the USS Repose were two of the most distinctive ships in the fleet. The USS Forrestal at 59,650 tons was the first of the US Navy's supercarriers, carrying a crew of 5000 sailors and 134 aircraft; it was hard to miss. The USS Repose was the world's only commissioned hospital ship in 1966. The USS Repose was only 11,141 tons, but it had a distinctive white hull with red crosses painted on port and starboard. It too was hard to miss. During my year on the USS Repose, the two ships met at sea three times. The first meeting was a source of humor. The second was ominous. The third meeting was tragic.

My first sighting of the mighty USS Forrestal was in October, 1966. The USS Repose was crossing the South China Sea on the way to Subic Bay in the Philippines. I finished my surgeries early and stepped out onto the weather deck to catch some sun and fresh air before lunch. On the horizon was a huge vessel heading toward the USS Repose at a rapid rate of speed. As the large vessel passed on our starboard side, I could appreciate how large and beautiful it was.

I heard one of the other officers say, "That's the Forrestal."

The USS Forrestal was heading in the opposite direction, back to Vietnam. As the two vessels passed each other, the bridge of the USS Forrestal flashed a message to our ship: "Who are you?"

The bridge officer on the USS Repose flashed back: "We are the USS Repose, AH-16. Who are you?" Our line officers thought the exchange was hilarious. The story quickly passed from one laughing officer to another.

The next time that I saw the USS Forrestal was different. It occurred in early 1967. A huge storm, Typhoon Nancy, was threatening the Western

Pacific and the 7th Fleet had been ordered to take shelter. The exception was the USS Repose, which had orders to return to Vietnam at ounce, crossing the sea in the mouth of the typhoon.

As the little USS Repose was leaving the security of the harbor, I saw another vessel rapidly heading into the safety of Subic Bay. It was quickly apparent from its size that it could only be the USS Forrestal. Seeing this massive, sea-worthy vessel seeking shelter while my ship was heading into the storm was ominous. It seemed obvious that my ship was on a fool's mission and taking risks with our safety. Within a few hours, the USS Repose was engulfed in the most ferocious storm I had ever seen. Our ship was tossed about by giant waves for two days. Most of the crew was too seasick to function. The old USS Repose listed so far port and starboard that I was sure we would capsize. Somehow, we did make to Vietnam intact, but the weather remained so bad that helicopter operations were cancelled and we were not able to receive any patients for two days.

On July 29, 1967, the staff of the USS Repose heard that the USS Forrestal had sustained a major disaster. A flight of loaded bombers had exploded on the flight deck and there had been severe damage and multiple casualties. Our ship had been ordered to proceed to Yankee Station at top speed to render assistance. We left Da Nang at top speed, but our World War II vessel took several hours to arrive at the scene of the tragedy. The surgeons had been directed to get some sleep while the USS Repose was underway. I was awakened at two a.m. and told to get to triage. Large helicopters from the USS Forrestal were landing on the flight deck and litter-bearers were bringing the victims into the triage area.

The first casualty to arrive was badly burned and obviously dead, so was the second, and the third, and on and on. We were receiving the dead victims before we saw any of the survivors.

The USS Repose had three frozen food lockers. The captain ordered one of the lockers to be emptied so the dead could be stacked in it. In the end, 134 dead sailors, most burned to a crisp, were stacked in the locker. Then, at last, the wounded began to arrive and were taken to surgery. What I saw were mostly shrapnel wounds from exploding bombs. Some of the victims said they were several decks below the flight deck and sleeping when they were injured. Not all of the 161 injured went to the USS Repose. Some were taken by other ships. All of the wounded who arrived on the USS Repose survived.

By mid-morning, all of my surgical patients were recovering and I went up to the weather deck to see what I could see. The scene was something that I had never encountered before. The USS Repose had been placed in a large formation of Navy vessels that was moving as one My ship was aft of the USS Forrestal. I was shocked to see the amount of damage to the mighty carrier. There was a huge hole in the stern, exposing the devastation that the ship had sustained.

The tragedy stayed with us for several days. The dentist from the USS Forrestal was transferred to our ship with the dental records of the missing sailors. Working with our two dentists, he was able to establish the identities of the badly burned corpses. I met him briefly in the wardroom and it was obvious from his vacant stare and his trembling hands he was a badly shaken man.

The USS Repose travelled south to Da Nang with one more mission. We tied up at the newly constructed dock to unload the bodies of our fallen sailors. It was an appalling sight to see. The dead in body bags were secured on wooden pallets, five to a pallet, and were unloaded by forklifts to begin their journey home. It was the most depressing scene I can recall from my time on board the USS Repose.

SANCTUARY

With the rest of the crew, I scanned the entrance to Da Nang harbor to see the new arrival. The USS Sanctuary, AH-17 had come from San Francisco, the second hospital ship in Vietnam. The Repose had been in country a few months earlier, but our sister ship underwent renovations before joining the Fleet. The new ship was white with red crosses port and starboard. It was the same design as the Repose but it had a new, larger flight deck. The officers and crew of our sister ship lined the deck, attired in Dress White uniforms as they sailed into Da Nang. I wondered how the arrival of this second hospital ship might affect my life in Vietnam. I enjoyed being part of the only hospital ship in country and arguably the best hospital in Vietnam. It had been amusing to be on the only ship in the US Navy to have women on board. Now, we would have to share those distinctions with the Sanctuary. I secretly believed that the new ship could not be as good as we were. Perhaps, my workload would decrease and I could catch up on my sleep. That would be good.

The senior officers of the Sanctuary and a number of the physicians paid us a visit via motor whaleboat. Our visitors, in Dress White uniforms, were welcomed in the Wardroom where a Welcome USS Sanctuary poster had been erected. A large flat-cake had been laid out, inscribed "Welcome USS Sanctuary to Vietnam." It seemed as if cake and coffee were the way that we celebrated everything. Liquor was not allowed on Navy ships. The Sanctuary physicians were eager to ask the Repose doctors what to expect. They bragged about their large flight deck and were surprised that the largest Marine helicopters had been landing on the smaller Flight Deck on the Repose, a tribute to the skill of the pilots.

Our little social hour was abruptly ended when a call for Flight Quarters rang out, on both ships. The Sanctuary doctors were quickly transported back to their vessel. I ran to the Flight Deck area with the other Repose doctors and crew. Two Marine APCs had hit mines and burst into flames causing severe burns to the troops riding inside. There were 24 casualties and half would be assigned to each ship. I realized that we could have gotten all 24 if the Sanctuary had not arrived.

After triage, all of our patients were taken to surgery, consisted of cleaning the wounds, removing dead tissue and applying dressings. Burns are the worst injuries. They are painful, disfiguring, and potentially fatal. They are even painful to look at. The most threatening aspect of burns in the early stage is management of fluid and electrolyte loss from the open burn wounds. Treatment required accurate replacement of fluid and electrolytes utilizing frequent laboratory evaluation and strict adherence to a proven formula. All of the burn patients would be admitted to the ICU. Larry Glass ordered that the four GMOs on the surgery services each spend 4 hours in the ICU during the night to make sure that fluid replacement was ideal.

The burn patients nearly filled the fifteen bed ICU. Two beds were taken by Marines with other injuries. There was one other patient in the unit, a North Vietnamese Lieutenant, a prisoner who had received injuries from a shotgun round to the face. His injuries were severe and included trauma to both eyes, resulting in blindness. I was curious about this enemy soldier. As I passed his bed I paused to see what the enemy looked like. He wore the same blue pajamas that all of our patients wore. He showed the same brave discipline in confronting his pain that is common with our Marines. He emitted no moans or cries of pain. He had suffered an injury from which he could never completely recover. I couldn't help but feel sorry for the guy.

My shift in the ICU was from ten PM to two AM. Checking on all of the lab reports, coming in on each patient every four hours, calculating the proper IV fluids, and writing the orders was more exhausting than doing surgery. I was fearful of making mistakes. It was nerve-wracking.

At about eleven PM, another person came into the unit. It was Father Coughlin, the Catholic Chaplain, who was working his way quietly from bed to bed and administering the Last Sacrament of his faith to the burned Marines who were Catholic. The sacrament is given to Catholics who are severely injured or gravely ill and in danger of dying. The prisoner began to cry out urgently. Sgt. Bill Tan, the Vietnamese interpreter was summoned and he arrived promptly. I stood bye to hear what the commotion was about. After a time, Sgt. Tan spoke to the small crowd of curious observers to say that the man told him that although he was blind and unable to see, he could tell from the sounds that there was a Catholic priest administering the sacrament and that he was Catholic and would like to receive the blessing. Father Coughlin administered the Sacrament of the Dying to the North Vietnamese Lieutenant. In a flash, I saw the paradox. It was the middle of the night. I was sleep-deprived and dead on my feet and working to keep my twelve burn patients alive but I had experienced the revelation that I had met the enemy and found that he was much like me.

ROCKETMAN

When the USS Repose was in the Da Nang area, a big part of my workload was debriding mortar wounds and removing the metallic fragments of the shells. This was very routine surgery which I was very comfortable with. Only a small amount of damaged or devitalized tissue was removed. The metal was found by placing my gloved finger into the wound and feeling around until I felt the fragment. To make things interesting, I indulged in a bit of showmanship with the operating room staff. I would request a "bullet forceps" from the scrub tech. I would be handed a large Kelly Clamp, which I used to grab the metal piece. Then I requested a "bullet bucket" from the circulating O.R. tech. The corpsman would hold the bucket handle so that the bucket was suspended next to the O.R. table. Then I would throw the metal fragment into the bucket with full force. If all went well, this would produce a loud *ding!* Everyone in the room would give a loud applause, and then the operation would go on. It was an amusing ritual, nothing more.

One evening in early 1967, a new weapon appeared in Da Nang. A heavy barrage hit the airbase. The first casualty was the officer's latrine. An Air Force captain was sitting on the can when a shell fragment struck him in his right buttock. He was rushed to the USS Repose while the attack was still underway. He became my patient and I took him straight to the operating room and prepared for surgery to debride his wound and remove the shell fragment. A stranger was present in the room, a Marine intelligence officer, tasked with determining what this new weapon was.

After cleaning and draping the buttock area, I explored the large wound and found that the damage was confined to the buttock muscles. Very little dissection was needed to get down to the metal fragment. I requested my bullet forceps and used it to grab the metal. The empty bucket was already in place, waiting for its prize. I pulled on the forceps, but nothing happened. The fragment didn't budge. I pulled harder, twisting the forceps this way and that. No movement. I reached into the wound, using my finger to try to free the muscles away from the fragment. I could feel that the piece was much larger than it had first appeared to be. I enlarged the incision, used a large periosteal elevator to separate the muscle and placed two retractors around the fragment, and then gave a mighty tug. The metal piece popped out of the buttock and was flung into the bucket. Instead of the usual ding there was a resounding *DONG!*

The intelligence officer grabbed the fragment from the bucket, studied it for a very short time, and pronounced it to be from a 135 millimeter, Russian made rocket, the first one in Vietnam.

I went out to the weather deck and could see the rockets still falling on Da Nang and aerial tracer bullets spraying the area of the rocket launchers. The battle was still going on and my patient was already out of surgery. That was my first rocket encounter.

My next experience with rockets occurred on the day when the USS Repose had its greatest excitement during my time on board. There was an early morning rocket attack on a Marine artillery unit near Dong Ha. A Marine was entering the command bunker with coordinates for return fire when a rocket followed him into the bunker and exploded. Six Marines were wounded and all were flown to the USS Repose for surgery. I was removing another rocket fragment when I heard the message "All hands prepare for collision." Then there was a huge metallic screech as the USS Repose collided with an oiler. My suturing became very rapid as damage control messages sounded over the PA. The crew saved the USS Repose and we headed to a dry dock in Subic for repairs.

My last brush with rockets was a strange one. The time came for my departure from Vietnam. I received orders to New London, my new duty station I went through the process of checking out on the ship. My replacement arrived. Finally, I received travel orders, leaving from Da Nang Airbase. I would be taken to Da Nang by boat after breakfast and transported to the airbase. The warrant officer offered advice to be sure to get an early flight as there would be a rocket attack at 1:30 a.m. The driver to the airbase also mentioned the expected rocket attack.

I checked in at the desk at the base to see when my flight would be. I had a choice of one p.m. flight to Clark in the Philippines for a five p.m. flight to southern California. The clerk also mentioned the expected 1:30 a.m. rocket attack. This attack must have been one of the worst secrets of the war. I opted for the five p.m.to California. My wife and new daughter were living in Oakland and this should work for me.

Unfortunately, the five p.m. plane kept getting delayed, first to eight, then to ten, then to 1:30 a.m. I had no option but to wait and hope. All the intended passengers waited outdoors, keeping an eye on the sky.

At about one a.m., a Boeing 707 glided into Da Nang, landed, and taxied to the terminal. The passengers quickly disembarked and the new passengers boarded. As soon as the seats were filled, we took off. As the plane was ascending, I looked down at the ground for any sign of rockets. I saw none.

About a month later, I met a corpsman who had missed my flight while having a few beers. He reported that there was a rocket barrage shortly after we took off. There was a lot of confusion and running around, but there appeared to be no casualties or serious damage.

PILOTS

Last year, I finally threw out my Marine flight suit, a gift from a patient fifty years ago. It had been useful in many home improvement projects, but the fabric was finally disintegrating.

In the spring of 1967, I was assigned two new patients with a different background from the majority of the casualties I had in the previous months. They were fighter-bomber pilots who had been shot down, recovered, and flown to the USS Repose. The two men arrived separately within the same month. Both had been injured while ejecting from their aircraft. Ejection from a falling jet was accomplished by firing a small explosive to blast the pilots seat through the canopy. This violent action caused a fracture of the right femur in one case and a compression fracture of the lumbar spine in the other. It was not surprising that being blasted out of a plane caused injuries. It was more puzzling that so few of my patients were pilots. There were a great number of aircraft lost in Vietnam, but death or captivity occurred more often than injury.

My two patients were housed in the rooms set aside for officers who were patients, a suite of semi-private rooms adjacent to the nurse's quarters. Both the injured pilots recovered quickly and were able to get back on their feet. Both tended to "accidentally" wander into the nurse's quarters.

Most of my contacts with pilots had occurred when the USS Repose was in Subic Bay for repairs. There was often a carrier in port and there were opportunities to meet pilots at the Officer's Club. Carrier pilots were a high-spirited bunch who were in a very dangerous profession. Just the basic functions of taking off and landing on a moving ship at sea were sometimes fatal. They had to deal with anti-aircraft fire on every mission. Between visits to Subic, each squad would lose members. It should not be a surprise that these pilots were known for hard partying.

There was a popular comic strip called "The Adventures of Buz Sawyer." Buz was a Navy aviator. In 1967, Buz was flying missions in Vietnam. The story had him wounded and flown to the USS Repose for surgery with Lt. Commander Rodney McDonald, with whom I was working. There was one frame of the comic showing Rod operating on Buz. There was one other un-identified surgeon depicted. I was the other doctor assisting Rod, but I wasn't named. However, I could brag that I was in the comics.

Sometimes the air war was close enough to shore that it could be observed from the USS Repose. I had seen a B-52 raid from such a distance that the aircraft were not visible. The effects of the bombs blowing up a moving path of destruction could not be missed.

In the fall of 1966, the USS Repose was sent south to Duc Pho to support a Marine operation against an enemy base camp. Some of the fighting was right on the coast. As the Marines were advancing, they had air support to bomb a group of bunkers. One A-4 was seen dropping its bomb and then crashing with a huge fireball and gasps from all of us who were watching.

In Subic Bay, there was one pilot who seemed to have a different role. People called him "Heavy Homer" or sometime just "Heavy." Funny thing was that he wasn't heavy at all. He was a normal sized lieutenant. The word was that he had once been heavy. He had shed the pounds, but the name stuck. Heavy was a mustang who had worked his way up through the ranks and was now a Navy pilot. He had a unique job. He was the representative for Navy pilots in the Western Pacific, handling all pilot complaints. He did his business poolside at the Cubie Point B.O.Q. Heavy Homer knew everything about the base and the personnel. He bragged about having the largest collection of Hei-neken beer in the Far East, stacked cases of the beer taking up one wall of his quarters. He once enticed one of our nurses to his room to view the beer. I'm not sure what happened after that, but the sturdy young lady left in such haste that she broke the doorknob off his door.

On the last afternoon of every odd numbered month, Heavy Homer flew from Cubie Point in the Philippines to Da Nang. On the morning of the first day of every even numbered month, he flew back to Cubie Point. In that way, he qualified for two months of combat pay. Heavy had it all figured out.

When the USS Repose was in Da Nang harbor, we anchored beneath the flight path for landings at the airbase. Pilots approaching their landings would fly low over the ship and bank their planes, trying to glimpse any nurses sunbathing on the upper deck. You had to see it to believe it.

When the USS Repose came to the aid of the USS Forrestal in the Summer of 1967, we received thirty-seven wounded and 134 dead sailors from the tragic explosion. None of the dead or wounded were pilots. The twenty-three pilots were all rescued by their crew chiefs. These highly trained fliers were too valuable to lose in an accident.

CARDIAC ARREST

During the time I was a medical student in the early 1960s, *Life Magazine* published an issue showing a group of interns running down a hospital corridor. The caption stated: "Why are these doctors running?" The lead story answered the question by describing a new concept in medical care known as "Code 99." The story focused on program at St. Vincent's Hospital in New York City. When a patient at the hospital exhibited signs of cardiac arrest, an announcement on the hospital intercom called out "Code 99" and gave the location of the emergency. All available physicians were summoned to quickly get to the location to assist in every possible measure to save the patient's life.

After completing medical school, I began an internship at St Vincent's and quickly became involved in the Code 99 program. A Code 99 involved activities to maintain circulation with closed chest cardiac massage, maintain respiration by intubation of the trachea, and use of ventilatory assist, installation of cardiac medication, and electric shock to restart the cardiac rhythm. It was a concerted effort to save a life and it had a high success rate.

As I had gone on in my medical career, I was involved in many cardiac arrest situations, usually successful in keeping patients alive. Occasionally, close chest massage does not succeed in maintaining circulation and it was necessary to open the chest and massage the heart directly.

The first time I encountered this problem was in my orthopedic residency. I was assisting a senior orthopedic surgeon in operating on a nineteen-year-old who had fractured two hips when he had leapt from a six-story roof thinking he could fly while on an LSD trip. The anesthesiologist called out that there was a cardiac arrest. We covered the hip incision and began chest compressions. Anesthesia reported that our efforts were not generating a carotid pulse and we would have to open the chest. My attending surgeon immediately handed me the scalpel, saying he had never opened a chest. I had never opened a chest either, but it wasn't a time to argue.

I took the knife and made a generous cut between the ribs on the left side of the patient's chest. I was able to reach into our patient's chest cavity very quickly and the heart was right where I expected it to be. I gave the organ a couple squeezes and could feel contraction of the cardiac muscle resume. Our anesthesiologist reported that a cardiac rhythm had returned and the carotid pulse had returned. After a time, we were able to get back to the hip repair.

A chest surgeon was called in to repair my chest incision. I was feeling proud of my work. The chest man looked at the left ribcage and called out, "Who made this incision?" I proudly sated that I had. He said, "You cut the nipple in half." I was a bit less proud of my work, but the patient survived with a unique scar to remind him of his indiscretion.

I'm sure other nipples have been bisected, but the only other case I'm aware of was done by another Dr. Walsh, my son, a medical resident in Utah, responding to a cardiac arrest in his ICU. You could say that we Walshes are nipple splitters.

I can only recall one cardiac arrest in my time on the USS Repose, but it was memorable. I was just completing a surgery in Operating Room #2, when the door of the O.R. opened and a corpsman stuck his head in and shouted, "Cardiac arrest in Room 1." I bolted out the door into the passageway, running toward the next O.R. Out of the corner of my eye, I could see another person in the space. He swerved to try to avoid me, but I bumped him while he was off-balance and he started to fall. As I dived through the door into Room #1, I could see the other man going down on his ass and noticed the two stars on his uniform. As I ran into the room to give my assistance, I realized I had just decked an admiral. The cardiac arrest was handled quickly. The best place for an arrest is an operating room because the equipment and personnel are readily available. I was not sure what my role was. Usually, I would start another major intravenous line for administering fluids and medication. As soon as everything was under control, I headed for the recovery room to see how my patient was doing.

Entering the recovery room, I spotted Admiral Lacey. He seemed to be uninjured and in good spirits. Wasting no time, I went to the admiral and offered my apologies.

"What for?"

"I knocked you down in the passageway," I explained.

The admiral faced me and said, "Lieutenant, you were doing your job and I was in the way. I should apologize to you."

I guess the lesson of this tale is if you knock an admiral on his ass, you had better have a good excuse, and it should be an admiral with a sense of humor.

SADNESS

"We'll fly you out to the Repose, and everything will be okay" Those were the words spoken to injured Marines being evacuated to my hospital ship.

There was truth in the statement in that the medical staff of the USS Repose was amazingly successful in saving the lives of the wounded. But not every survivor was okay. Many lived but lost something important as result of their wounds. The physical wounds were usually obvious. Emotional injuries could be more subtle. For some, in their minds, the war was never-ending.

As a surgeon, I saw the price paid in a direct way. It was, in a real way, the things they left behind that would be missed for the duration of their lives. Missing arms and legs were obvious. Missing intestinal segments or brain tissue were not as visible. Nerve damage and vascular defects would be problematic for life. At one time, the medical staff debated whether it was worth saving a life if the injuries would hamper the ability to have a normal life. The outcome of that discussion was we would endeavor to save every life and to hope for a good outcome over time.

An extreme example was the case of Lt. Spivey, who had been wounded by a Claymore mine. Almost every part of his body was injured. He lost an enormous amount of blood, more blood than he had in his body. Transfusions kept him alive while every surgical service operated on his injuries: neurosurgery, ophthalmology, ENT, thoracic surgery, abdominal surgery, urology, and orthopedics. The surgeons removed damaged brain, one eye, several feet of intestine, one testicle, and one leg below the knee. The lieutenant was several days in a coma, and then he began to recover. He regained enough strength to be medivacked home to the states.

A few weeks later, a letter arrived addressed to the medical staff of the USS Repose from a Doctor Spivey, the father of the lieutenant thanking us warmly, for saving his son and reporting that he was doing well. It was good to hear that, but I knew his life would be changed in so many ways. That was the source of my sadness.

Of all the patients I treated in Vietnam, the one who has given me the most painful memories was a Marine Sergeant who had been shot in his knee and sustained a vascular injury to his popliteal artery, the major blood supply to the lower leg. The Sergeant was an African American, powerfully built, tall, and handsome. He had been taken to NSA DaNang Hospital where the surgeons attempted a vascular repair of the damaged artery. The repair failed and he was in danger of developing gangrene. He was then transferred to the USS Repose for another repair of the artery.

I was assigned to assist Dr. Frank Gorman with the surgery. Even at the start of surgery, things looked bad the leg was cool and dusky-colored. Dr. Gorman re-opened the incision behind the knee and found that there was no blood flow through the artery and gangrene was evident below and above the knee. The leg could not be saved. The next step would be to amputate the leg above the knee to prevent the gangrene from taking his life.

The amputation was my surgery. I divided the femur with a saw and the muscle and skin flaps were closed. He was taken to the recovery room, still asleep from the anesthesia. I waited by the Sergeant's side for him to wake up. When I was convinced he was alert, I faced him to tell him what had happened. Bracing myself, I told him we weren't able to save his leg and had to amputate the leg above the knee. I added that he would be evacuated to the Navy Prosthetic Center in San Diego where he would be fitted with a prosthetic leg and he would be instructed in how to walk with it.

The Sergeant digested my words and paused to consider how to respond. After a while, he looked me in the face and said, "Doc, tell me this, what good is a one-legged Nigger in South Carolina?"

I had no answer for the Sergeant's question.

ENSIGN HAN

A case I can't forget is that of Ensign Han. During the conflict, I performed 770 surgeries. Of those thirty-two were laparotomies, opening, exploring, and repairing damage done to the abdominal contents caused by penetrating wounds, usually from gunshots. These procedures were more challenging than extremity injuries. The three doctors on my surgical service, "Tiger Service," took turns performing and assisting on them.

It so happened that it was my turn when a young Korean Marine, Ensign Han, was brought to the USS Repose after sustaining a bullet wound to his belly. He was in his early twenties and, like all Korean Marines, was extremely fit. Or at least he appeared to be. He had a small entry wound in his anterior abdominal wall. No exit wound was found on him. An abdominal X-ray did not show any bullet. His blood count was low as was his blood pressure, consistent with internal bleeding. It would have been convenient to have an MRI to show where the bullet tracked, but MRI had not yet been invented. It was easy to see where a bullet entered, but its path within the body could be hard to predict.

I ordered blood cross-matched and prepared our man for surgery. For this patient, I used a scalpel to create a large, midline incision extending from the ribcage to the pelvis in several layers, clamping and cauterizing bleeders as I went. Once the abdomen was fully opened, retractors were placed so I could gain access to the abdominal contents. It was immediately evident there was a large amount of bleeding coming from the liver. I controlled this with packing, and the rest of the cavity was carefully explored. This was necessary to ensure there was no penetration of the bowel which would lead to sepsis. The entire intestine had to be "run," picked up, and inspected. No lesions were found. The kidneys, spleen, and pancreas were okay. It was time to address the liver injury.

Gunshot wounds of the liver are always serious because the liver is a large, highly vascular organ. The larger vessels could be clamped and ligated or cauterized, but there were numerous small vessels which could continue to bleed profusely. Carefully bringing the wound edges together was the best way to control this bleeding. However, surgeons have found the liver to be difficult to sew. The tissue is delicate and sutures could cut through it like a hot knife through butter.

Larry Glass, my immediate superior and my assistant on this case, had taught me his technique for repairing livers. We used thicker sutures to avoid cutting through the tissue and carefully putting just enough tension on the knot to bring the organ edges together. Inspection revealed that the bullet entered at the anterior aspect of the lower border of the liver and continued toward the proximal dome. There was a gaping hole in the organ, but it was a clean wound with very little devitalized tissue and no visible bullet fragments.

I began the repair by doing a limited debridement of non-viable tissue. All large bleeders were clamped and cauterized. Then I began carefully suturing the edges of the wound together, using a heavy, chromic catgut suture on a large needle, and avoiding excessive tension on the suture. The repair process was proceeding toward the dome of the liver. I was starting to feel relieved that the end was in sight. I couldn't have been more wrong! As I placed my last suture in the dome of the liver, a frightening site caught my attention. Just above the exit wound in the liver was a small, round hole in the diaphragm. The bullet had entered the chest cavity in the area occupied by the heart. The bullet track was somewhat anterior. It possibly missed the heart. There was no way to know without exploring the chest cavity.

Larry was an experienced cardio-thoracic surgeon and would do that part of the operation while I assisted. I closed the abdomen in layers, prepped the chest, and re-draped. Larry made an incision in the anterior chest used a saw to split the sternum and retracted the wound edges to expose the chest cavity. There was another small, round hole in the pericardium, the fibrous sack covering the heart. Opening the pericardium, the heart was easily inspected. The myocardium, the heart muscle, was un-scathed, but there was another problem. The blood supply to the heart is delivered via the coronary arteries and the major artery is the anterior, descending coronary, and that vessel had been cleanly divided by the bullet. The ensign had been dealt a heart attack.

Today, coronary bypass surgery using an operating microscope and vein grafts, is routinely successful. In my time in Vietnam, the technique was not available. Our young patient struggled to survive, but the twin burdens of a liver wound and myocardial infarction were too much to overcome. After four difficult days, he died.

THE MONTAGNARD

I was called to the operating room at two p.m. A new patient had arrived from the Special Forces unit at Lan Vei. He had been severely wounded while defending the base. The Special Forces officers had sent him to the USS Repose for treatment because he had fought bravely. The patient was a Montagnard tribesman. He was small and wiry, dark-skinned, and dressed in a loin cloth. He had two remarkable injuries from AK-47 rounds. One bullet entered through his left ear and exited through his nose, causing loss of most of the nose. The second round grazed his anterior abdominal wall, resulting in evisceration (spilling out) of the intestines. Strangely, his Montagnard colleagues had attempted to cover the intestines by creating a cocoon of mud and leaves. I was assigned to treat the abdominal wound and Gerry Verdi, an aspiring plastic surgeon, would attempt to reconstruct the nose.

My surgery on this fellow consisted of a thorough washing to remove the dirt and leaves. After the area was satisfactorily cleaned, I inspected the abdominal contents. Finding no internal injuries, I closed the abdominal wound. The head injury was more severe. The bullet, in passing from the ear to the nose, damaged the two optic nerves causing major blindness in the left eye and partial blindness in the right eye. Chances for recovery of sight were not good. Gerry was able to repair the nose, but the result was a somewhat diminished appendage resembling a pig's snout.

The Montagnard was not sent to the international ward as he could not speak or understand Vietnamese. He was given a bed on the Tiger Ward with our Marine patients. He was a blind man, placed in a room where nobody could speak his language. The isolation and depression of this man who couldn't see his surroundings and couldn't understand those around him must have been severe. He sat quietly, day after day, waiting for something to happen.

Amazingly, he did not develop any abdominal infection, although he had suffered gross contamination of the abdomen. The Marines in the ward complained that the Montagnard gnashed his teeth while he slept every night. That was the only way he expressed his distress.

At that time, I purchased a box of Philippine cigars to celebrate the birth of my daughter. They weren't very good cigars and I couldn't get anyone to smoke one. In desperation, I offered a cigar to the Montagnard. He lit it up and seemed to love it. I gave him the whole box.

Every afternoon, his corpsman would wheel him out to the weather deck, light up his cigar, and watch some signs of pleasure appear on his face. When our man was transferred back to Lang Vei, he took the remainder of the cigars with him. I hoped that he would have some return of his vision and future happiness. The following year, the North Vietnamese overran our base in Lang Vei, using tanks for the first time.

THE ENEMY

My time on the Tiger Service provided me with an invaluable surgical experience which would serve me well for the rest of my career. However, I had decided to specialize in orthopedic surgery. I knew I would be wise to see if I could spend some time on the orthopedic service.

I spoke with Captain Snyder, requesting a transfer to the orthopedic service. He promised me I could transfer to ortho when Royce Hansen would be leaving. In the meantime, I could work with the ortho guys whenever I had time. Rod MacDonald was our orthopedic surgeon. He was horribly over-worked.

A hospital of our size in a war zone should have had several orthopedists. Rod was assisted by Royce, a GMO, like myself. Rod was trained as a hand surgeon and was used to doing neat and dainty repairs of hands and fingers. The gross trauma cases he had to deal with in Vietnam horrified him. His expression on seeing each new case was, "This is the worst one yet."

As soon as Rod heard that I intended to be an orthopedist, he assumed I was another orthopedist and I was ready to lighten his load. That evening, he consulted me in the operating room where I was finishing a case. He told me there was a patient in Room 2, needing knee surgery. The fact that I had had very limited training in orthopedics didn't bother him. He told me the patient was a young lady with a swollen, painful knee probably from a torn meniscus. He advised me to make a median, para-patella incision and remove the tear. He added that the woman was an enemy combatant. Rod then went into Room 3 to perform another surgery on a trauma.

I was uneasy about taking on an operation I wasn't completely familiar with, but I felt that this was my opportunity to show I could be an orthopedist.

I did know enough to make the medial, para-patella incision, but then things got complicated. As I opened the knee, fluid and multiple small, white, fleshy particles floated out. I had no idea what I had gotten into.

Ron was summoned to Room 2. He took a quick look and pronounced, "Tuberculosis! Do a synovectomy, put in a drain, and start her on Streptomycin."

I followed his directions and the case went okay.

When the young lady awoke from anesthesia, she gave me a look I had never seen on a patient before. It was a look of pure hatred. I realized that, to her, I represented the enemy. Still, she was my patient and I owed her my best care. She seemed to be doing well after he surgery and antibiotics. Then, she developed a new problem, a hip abscess. I had to take her back to the O.R. to drain the lesion. The look of hate continued. Finally, she was doing well enough to be transferred to the Vietnamese hospital. I went to the international ward to discharge her. She began to shout in Vietnamese and the translator had to be called. Sergeant Bill Tang listened to her, and then turned to me to say that she wanted to thank me very much for all that I had done for her. I told the Sergeant to tell her that I wished her well and the war would someday end and we could both go back to our lives.

AN NA

I am An Na. I am now an old woman, but once I was a young soldier in the Peoples' Army during the American War. I will tell you how I came to be a patient on the American Hospital Ship during that time.

My husband, Tran Vong, and I lived in the village of Gia Lin, which was on Highway 1 and just below the Demilitarized Zone. Our area was always close to military action, even during the French War, but more so with the division of our country. We had been happy in Gia Lin. It was a beautiful place, near the sea with rolling hills and fertile farms. My husband was a fisherman who took his narrow boat out into the South China Sea to fish whenever the weather was safe. We had a small farm that produced more than enough rice and vegetables for us and our two small children. Then, the shelling and bombing of our area became too much to bear. First, my husband and then I joined the liberation forces (Viet Cong) to help free our country from the conflict and drive away the American invaders. My husband's parents took in our son and daughter while Tran was away fighting. Like other women, I worked on supply and intelligence.

The work was very hard. Heavy supplies had to be carried to our fighting men in the hills. Because we had to avoid American patrols, we usually worked at night. I was always tired. I couldn't get enough sleep. When I did sleep, I often woke up drenched in perspiration. I rarely was able to see my husband and children. Although I ate all my rations, I was becoming very slender. My clothing became loose on me and my bones were showing. The worst thing was the pain in my right knee, which was worse every day. The knee became swollen and it caused difficulty with walking. I was becoming a sick woman.

One morning, when I was in Quang Tri City to get supplies, my knee collapsed causing me to fall in the street. I tried to get back on my feet, but I was unable to do so. The police were called to help me. They seemed uncertain about what to do. One of the policemen remembered that an American doctor was in Quang Tri that day and they said they would take me to be seen by him. I was terrified about being seen by an American. I hated the Americans. They had brought war to our country and killed many of my friends.

However, the American doctor I saw was a kind man. He examined my knee carefully and then spoke to his female assistant, who explained to me in Vietnamese that I needed treatment for the knee. They would take me in a helicopter to an American ship that would give me the care I needed. This was very disturbing news. I hated and feared the Americans and had never before been on a helicopter or a ship.

Everything happened quickly. We landed on a white American ship. Two sailors carried me into the ship. I felt like I was a prisoner of the enemy. I was placed in a bed and a large needle was stuck in my arm and liquid flowed through it. I didn't know what was happening to me. Then, another American doctor came to examine me. He seemed young and not very sure of himself. He indicated he was "Bac Si Walsh." He was normal-sized. He had a red face and blue eyes and wore green pajamas with no sleeves and a funny little hat. Using an interpreter, he told me that something was wrong inside of my knee and that he would do an operation to fix the problem. I did not have confidence in this young doctor, but I knew that the knee had to be fixed.

I had a long sleep after the surgery. When I awoke, I had more pain in the knee than I had before. I was certain that something had gone wrong. I had been placed in a room that was crowded with Vietnamese patients of all ages: children, adults, and soldiers. The nurse was Asian, but she only spoke American. Bac Si Walsh came to visit me with the interpreter. They told me that the knee had a bad infection and would need a long treatment. I believe that the doctor could tell I hated him; I could not hide the expression on my face. But he was gentle and polite. He still seemed uncertain of what he was doing. I think that my knee condition was worse than he had suspected.

Bac Si visited me every day, changing the bandage on my knee, checking on the plastic tube coming out of the knee, and reading the records of my case. He took the sutures out of my incision and tested the knee for movement.

One week after I had been on the American ship, a new problem arose. I developed a painful swelling in the right hip. This time the Bac Si seemed to know what to do. He quickly produced a giant needle and syringe. With no warning, he stuck the needle into the swelling and drew out a large amount of thick, white fluid. Strangely, this brutal treatment relieved my pain. He told me I would have to undergo another operation to get the rest of the infection out of the hip. I understood and agreed to have the procedure. I was beginning to trust Bac Si more.

My second surgery was not too bad. I had been getting medication for my infection (which I had been told was tuberculosis) and I was feeling much better. I began to gain weight, even with the strange American food. The American doctor was pleased with my progress. Through the interpreter, he informed me that I would need continuing treatment and I would be transferred to the Vietnamese hospital in Da Nang. I was happy to hear this. In Da Nang, I might be able to see my children and maybe even my husband. He turned to leave, but I yelled for the interpreter and asked him to tell the Bac Si I was grateful for care he had given me.

These things happened many years ago, but they remain in my memories. I am sorry I hated Bac Si Walsh. We were both affected by the awful war that caused our peoples to hate each other. Things in my country are different now. My husband did not survive the war, but my children did and they both speak American English and are happy to converse with the many American visitors who now come to our country in peace.

LOSS

Lieutenant Curtis Baker was an outstanding representative of the US Navy Medical Corps. He was tall, almost 6 feet, athletic, handsome and enthusiastic. He dressed smartly in well-pressed fatigues and was always ready with a winning smile. Curtis was nominally a Marine Flight Surgeon. What he actually did was somewhat more. His mission was to fly into the villages of Quang Tri Provence to indentify the health care needs of these under-served areas and to try to help the people to obtain medical care. He was very effective at providing help to the villages. When he found a Vietnamese needing special care, such as cardiac surgery, he would bring the person to our ship. He was well-known to the Repose Medical Staff. More than any person that I knew, Curtis seemed to enjoy his time in Vietnam.

Curtis was popular with the Repose doctors. He was friendly and could tell a good story. He was always welcome to lunch in our Wardroom. Curtis travelled with his Vietnamese interpreter, Anh Tran. She was petite and pretty, with the small facial features and high cheek-bones common to her race. She wore fatigues of a camouflage material that were nearly skin-tight, displaying her attractive shape. She also wore a stylish, Australian-style campaign hat. Ahn was always close by Curtis's side and her eyes were constantly on him. If Curtis turned to Ahn, he would show a warm smile. I don't know if the two of them shared a romance, but I hoped that they did. They seemed so good together.

On each visit, Curtis would ask us if we had any particular kind of cases that we'd like to have transferred to our service. On one occasion, I asked about thyroid tumors. On his next visit Joe came with three ladies, each having a goiter as big as a baseball! Jim MacGowan had an interest in cancer of the penis. Four unfortunate men with penis cancer arrived with the next batch of patients. Rick DuBoise had a request for patients with liver abscess. He was rewarded with two. It was professionally pleasing to have some variety in our work. How Curtis was able to find so many patients with rare conditions was a mystery. He was also able to provide a steady supply of Vietnamese patients for our heart surgery program.

Curtis and Ahn visited the Repose about once a month. They were always welcome. Aside from the professional relationship that we shared, they had become friends. Somehow, during those visits, I never got around to talking with Curtis about his life before Vietnam or his plans for the future. I guess that we were too occupied with the present business of taking care of our patients.

I don't know how the news reached us, but one morning I heard the shocking news that Curtis Baker had been killed. It seemed impossible that Curtis could be dead. He had been, I thought, invincible. The word was that he had volunteered to go along on a Recon flight over the DMZ on March 28, 1967.His helicopter was shot down. The entire crew perished. Ahn was not with him when he died. It made no sense for Curtis to be flying on such a dangerous mission. Doctors working with the Marines can fall into the trap of acting more like Marines, and less like doctors. We will now never know now how Curtis would use his talents to help people. We will never know if Curtis and Ahn could have found happiness together.

The operation that Curtis Baker had been running was shut down when he died. No replacement was found to take his place. The translator on the Repose, Sargent Bill Tang was leaving. Ahn applied for his position, but it went to another Vietnamese woman. It was rumored that our nurses had vetoed Ahn.

The death of Curtis Baker was a loss, just one of the 58,000 young Americans who lost their lives in this beautiful, but troubled country, so far from their homes.

STOWAWAY

J ust before the evening meal, Lt. Stone, the engineering officer, handed me an envelope. It was from Captain Campbell and it contained a request for me to attend Captains Mast the next morning at ten. I was ordered to represent one of my patients being tried for absence without official leave (AWOL). Captains Mast is a legal proceeding carried out on a ship. It is a form of Court Marshall. I was being commanded to act as an attorney for a Marine who was a patient on my service. This was a new, and somewhat upsetting, development. I was not a lawyer and didn't know much about the law. I didn't know anything about the case.

After dinner, I went to the ward to interview the accused, Lance Corporal Tyrone Jones. I remembered that he had arrived by helicopter with a large number of Marines who had been wounded in an artillery barrage at Con Thein. He was a small, young Black man with upper and lower extremity shrapnel wounds. He was quiet and polite, a good patient. I asked the lance corporal what had happened that he had charges placed against him.

The young man told me his story. He and some of his buddies were able to get leave for the evening to visit Olongapo. They found their way to the Leatherneck Club on the main drag. It was the usual setup with a band, waiters, drinks, and "hostesses." He hadn't been with any female in a long time and went a little crazy with Connie Dominques, the first girl he met there. They had drinks, danced, and chatted. She was very quick to offer him an "overnight" for "thirteen pesos only;" about four dollars. He accepted and spent the night with Connie. He had somehow forgotten that he was supposed to be back on the USS Repose by midnight.

Tyrone was able to make it back to the ship in the morning. He tried to find a way to get aboard without being noticed. On the pier, he saw a few sailors busy loading baskets of laundry onto the USS Repose. Seeing his chance, he snuck around behind some equipment to where the baskets were sitting. He removed some of the laundry bales from one basket and tucked his small frame into the bottom of the basket and pulled three bales of laundry on top of him. In short order, he felt the basket rise as he was heading back to the USS Repose. Then, he felt the basket drop to the pier. The two sailors lifting his bucket noted that it was heavier than the others and they stopped to investigate. They found the little Marine hiding in the bottom and reported him.

I liked Lance Corporal Tyrone Brown and I admired his plot, even if it wasn't successful. I felt as if the sailors who discovered him lacked a sense of humor. Of course, he was guilty of the charges and would face some punishment. As defense attorney, I would do what I could to help him.

The following morning, the trial was held in the captain's office. Lieutenant Stone was the prosecutor and spoke first, repeating the story about the laundry basket that was too heavy and asking for a guilty verdict. The captain then asked me to speak for the accused. I rose and addressed the captain, asking for leniency. I noted that the lance corporal was only nineteen years old, had been in fierce combat, and had been decorated with a Bronze Star and a Purple Heart in his short carrier as a Marine.

The captain left the office briefly to consider the testimony. In a few minutes, he returned to pronounce, "Lance Corporal Brown, I find you guilty of being absent without official leave. Your punishment will be confinement to quarters, reduction in rank, and forfeiture of pay."

That was the end of the proceedings.

My first and last case as a lawyer, and I had failed completely. I faced Tyrone Brown and apologized for the poor result. He was unfazed and told me not to worry because the Marine Corps always threw out the Navy punishments against Marines.

HOMEWARD BOUND

In July, 1967, I received orders that I would be relieved from duties in Vietnam and would be returning to the United States, proceeding to my new duty station in New London, CT. What would it feel like to be home? I had a new wife and a new daughter in Oakland, California. Being united with them was a big part of returning home. But California was not my home and I would be there for only a short time.

Finally, my replacement had arrived and I was leaving the USS Repose. On the day before my departure, Captain Snyder called me to his office to wish me well and to give me a letter of commendation. He was joined by Commander Larry Glass. Gerry Verdi had already left the USS Repose to return to his surgical residency at Columbia-Presbyterian Hospital.

After breakfast, while the rest of the medical staff was returning to their work in the wards or the operating rooms, I boarded a motor whale boat and a boatswains-mate transported me a and my suitcase from the ship to Da Nang, the first step in going home. Leaving the USS Repose after the year I had there was the hardest part of the trip home. I did have feelings of guilt for departing before the job was done. I would miss my friends and the incredible work that we were doing.

Arriving at the Da Nang airbase, I was able to secure a flight to Southern California, heading home. The flight left just before a rocket attack on the base. We stopped for breakfast and refueling in Okinawa and then took off for California, my temporary home. When the sky was getting dark, the pilot announced, "Gentlemen, we are now over the coast of California." The entire plane erupted in applause. We were sort of home.

From Vandenberg Airforce base, I took a bus to LAX and booked a flight to Oakland. I was surprised at how anti-military American Airlines seemed, charging all the returning veterans full fare and not serving breakfast to anyone in uniform. I didn't use that airline for another twenty years after that experience.

I did get to Oakland and was met by my young wife, Nancy, at the airport. We had gotten married before my deployment and had spent most of our first year of marriage apart. We had enjoyed a few days together in Hong Kong during the "Christmas truce." Nancy said that she was too excited and too nervous to drive. I hadn't driven in one year and hadn't slept in twenty-four hours, but I drove our MG from the airport to our apartment in the seventy-mile per hour bumper-to-bumper traffic on the Nimitz Freeway. Arriving at the apartment, I met my new daughter, Colleen, for the first time. What a thrill! Life would never be the same again.

The next part of the journey would be returning east. We would drive the three thousand-miles in our MG with Colleen in a bassinette behind our seats. It was summer and we didn't have air conditioning, but the trip was fun crossing the U.S.A. and seeing what a beautiful country I had returned to. We passed through Las Vegas, Yellowstone, and the farms of the Midwest. And we did it as a family. It did feel like I was almost home.

We were on our way to my new duty station in New London, CT. The plan was to stop and spend a day with Nancy's parents in Hackensack, N.J., and another day with my family in Valhalla. Hackensack was home for Nancy and she was happy to see her parents and her siblings. Everybody made a fuss about little Colleen. It was a nice visit.

The next morning, we crossed the Hudson and headed to Westchester. I immediately felt more comfortable on the New York side of the river. Familiar sites greeted me every mile along the parkway. I was delighted to see that my little hometown had not visibly changed. The same family-run businesses occupied the buildings on Broadway, the only commercial street in the village. When we stopped at 155 Prospect Ave, home address for almost all of my life, my heart must have skipped a beat. I was home! The old Victorian building with the wrap-around porch greeted us. My mother rushed to the door and gave me a huge hug. She had been consumed by the anguish of having two sons in Vietnam. Now, one was home. She greeted Nancy warmly and delighted in little Colleen.

My parents had organized a big cook out celebration to welcome me and my little family. I was the oldest of ten children and all of my brothers and sisters were coming to Valhalla to welcome me home, all except Nick who was still in the Central Highlands of Vietnam. There is nothing like the feeling of being welcomed by a really big family. My father manned the barbecue and my mother supplied her usual feast of her traditional favorites. Neighbors stopped by to offer their greetings.

Afterwards, Dad organized a backyard softball game, a family tradition, fiercely contested and great fun. The party lasted into the night. I couldn't have felt more at home.

The next morning Nancy and Colleen and I got back into the MG to head for New London to find a new home at my next duty station.

SAINT VINCENT'S

The neighborhood looked as I remembered it. It was the same colorful Greenwich Village that had been my home for two years, before my entering service in the Navy. As I approached the main entrance to Saint Vincent's Hospital on 11th Street, it seemed to be unchanged. When I walked through the doors, I began to detect a change, not a visible change, but a feeling that things were different. The clerk at the entrance asked if he could help me. That was a change. Before I left, everyone in the hospital knew me.

The African American security man leaned toward the clerk, and said, "That's Dr. Walsh."

I barely recognized the security man, but we glanced at each other and nodded. I suspected that he knew where I was coming from.

I walked aimlessly down the corridor of St. Joseph's Hall, passing the alcove with the statue of St. Joseph. Legend had it that a little intern named Leo Sullivan had too much to drink one evening and passed out. Before he came to, his fellow interns wrapped him in a body cast, removed St. Joseph, and placed the immobilized Leo in his place. The nuns found him there in the morning on their way to mass.

I kept passing young interns and residents, going about their chores. It was a familiar site, but their faces were fresh and unfamiliar to me. Wanting to find someone I knew, I headed up to the doctor's lounge next to the operating room suite. When I got there it was empty, but I poured myself a cup of coffee and sat down. Within a few minutes, a familiar face appeared. It was Bob Mackey who had been an intern and junior resident with me. He was between surgeries and wearing his scrubs. He greeted me warmly, poured himself a coffee, and sat down. We both had a lot of questions for the other and we had a few minutes to get them answered.

I started first, asking what was happening to the program and the doctors I had been working with. Bob quickly informed me that everything was changing. All the male house staff, without deferment, had gone into the military, even those with health problems. Dr. Louis Rousselot had left for Washington to become the under-secretary of defense. The new chairman was making changes in the surgical training, focusing more on the management of surgical patients and less on operative technique. I couldn't get enthused about that new direction. I was "old school" and was more interested in the surgery itself.

When I left, Bob and I had both been second year residents. In this "pyramid" program, only two of the starting eight residents would go on to become chief resident. Bob told me that he and Tom Higgins had been selected to be the senior resident and they expected to be the chiefs next year. They were both good men and I expected that they would do a fine job, but they did not seem likely to be promoted had it not been for the number of house staff leaving for the military. Bob told me about what cases he had been doing, and I politely congratulated him, though his caseload was much lighter than mine had been in Vietnam. I realized that Bob was where I would have been if I had not joined the Navy.

Then Bob asked about what my experience had been in Vietnam. I was surprised and stunned by the question. I found it very difficult to even begin discussing Vietnam with someone who hadn't been there. I was ducking questions, using broad generalities. I did explain that I was mainly performing surgery on a ship and was in a safe place. I said that it was "busy." I was reluctant at that point to reveal the secrets of my experience to a civilian, even one who is a physician. How could I tell him how I had amputated the shattered leg of a Marine with a straight razor, or performed a difficult emergency splenectomy or witnessed the bodies of 134 sailors being removed from my ship with a fork-lift. These things had to remain inside of me for a time. I just told Bob I did a lot of things and saw a lot of things.

Bob had to leave me to perform his next operation. It had been two years since I had last seen him, two years for both of us, but I felt that I had gained more experience and surgical maturity in that time, but I realized that, in a way, I had aged more than he had.

THE IMPOSTER

In many of the stories of military service, a big part of the narrative is focused on the struggle of surviving basic training, common to all branches of the military. The physical and mental challenges to survive this period of harassment is something that is vividly recalled by military people. The shrill drill Sergeant, the forced marches, the endless inspections, and the verbal abuse in all services seem to be necessary to turn civilians into military personnel.

Perhaps, it was because I never had to endure basic training of any kind, I never felt that I was truly a military person. When I entered the Navy, the service had a need for the skills that I had acquired in civilian life, surgeon. Basic training in my case consisted in watching instructional movies for two days and practicing my salute with a chief petty officer. I don't regret missing out on the rigors of basic training, but I did feel that my rank of lieutenant was cheaply earned. I felt like I was a civilian masquerading as a Navy officer.

On my third day in the Navy, I received orders to proceed to Fairfield, California to begin transportation to the USS Repose. The trip was slow with more stops than seemed necessary: Hawaii, Wake Island, Subic Bay, Cam Rahn Bay, Da Nang, Dong Ha, and, finally, the USS Repose. Once on board, I was basically in a hospital, an environment that I was familiar with. I didn't have to be too military. I was working with other doctors, who didn't even try to be military. The Navy didn't care. Doctors always got a pass on military etiquette. When the physicians on the USS Repose refused to follow the Navy rule of wearing a hat when outdoors, the captain issued a rule that no person on the USS Repose could wear a hat outdoors (because of aircraft operations).

My next duty station was the little Navy hospital at New London, CT. I was welcomed there and given whatever I requested. My Vietnam experience was a plus. The facility in Groton, was a submarine base. Submariners were as different from Marines as could be. They were brainy and very quiet. Work there was busy, but much less frantic than crazy Vietnam. I was made assistant director of orthopedic surgery, even though I hadn't done an orthopedic residency. The director, Bob Jung, hadn't completed his training either, but he was an excellent surgeon, and we had doctors from submarines with us when they were in port. It was a good time for my professional development.

I was approaching the end of my two-year commitment to the Navy Medical Corps. I had no demands on me to act like a military person. I had never fired a weapon or marched. I had never stood for inspection. My thoughts were on returning to civilian life and the resumption of surgical residency. Then, word came of a change of command in the hospital. The new commander was said to be a "spit and polish" Navy man. Soon after arriving, our new commander ordered a full dress inspection for all the medical personnel, dress whites with medals and swords!

I knew that I would have to comply with this order. I had purchased a set of dress whites which I hadn't yet used. I had been awarded four medals. How did I get four medals? Of course, I had no sword and I didn't think that a non-combatant should have to carry a sword. There were number of line officers in my apartment complex and I was able to borrow a sword from one of them. Perhaps, I could pull this inspection off.

The day of the inspection was a regular work day and I was seeing patients up until the time of the ceremony. Jim Howard, the least military of the doctors, who had gained too much weight to fit into his uniform, was assigned to man the clinic while the rest of the medical staff quickly changed into dress uniforms and hurried to the parade grounds. I took my place in the line of splendidly attired Naval officers and stood at attention.

Our new captain slowly walked down the line, sternly surveying each officer before moving on to the next. When he came to me, the captain paused for a very long time, looked me up and down and gravely pronounced, "Lieutenant, your sword is on backwards."

As he moved past me, I looked to my right and to my left. Every other sword was facing backwards and mine was facing forwards. My only inspection of my life and I failed. For two years I had pretended to be a proper Navy man and I almost pulled it off!

SERGEANT RILEY

Several years ago, I was testifying in court. It wasn't a big case. It was a simple injury matter. As the treating physician, I had to give testimony about the injuries sustained, the treatment, and the residual disability. Easy! After my testimony was completed, I was done and started to step down from the witness stand. The judge in the case, Judge Riley, leaned toward me and asked if we could speak. I replied that we could.

The judge looked me in the face and, after a short while, asked, "Doctor Walsh, do you remember me?"

I tried to recall ever meeting a Judge Riley in any prior court appearance, but I came up blank.

The judge was quiet for a moment, and then asked, "Do you member when I was Sergeant Riley, United States Marine Corps?"

I was stunned! My memory raced back to a time more than thirty years before.

I had completed two years of military service in Vietnam and at the Naval Hospital in New London. I returned to complete my residency training. One of my first rotations was at the Manhattan VA Hospital. On my first day at the VA, the chief resident, Ivan, led the junior residents (of which I was one) on rounds of the inpatients. He stopped at the bed of one patient and announced, "This is Sergeant Riley, United States Marine Corps. He has an infected non-union of his right tibia from a gunshot wound in Vietnam. We're going to do a below knee amputation on him tomorrow."

I was horrified. Ivan was my chief resident, but what he was planning was wrong. I said, "Ivan, we don't have to amputate. I treated a lot of these injuries in the Navy."

Ivan was annoyed by my criticism, but he replied, "Okay, Walsh, you take care of him."

Junior residents are not supposed to operate without the supervision of attending physicians or approved chief residents, but no one stopped me from bringing Sergeant Riley to the O.R. and repairing his wounded leg. I had been doing surgery in the Navy for two years. The procedure that Sergeant Riley had was simple. I merely cleaned and debrided the leg wound, shortened the leg slightly, and applied a walking cast. He seemed to be doing well when I left the VA for my next rotation.

The judge seemed eager to tell me what had happened since we last saw each other. He told me of a young lady, a lawyer who was a volunteer at the VA. They fell in love and married. He credited his wife with getting him to finish high school, attend college, and graduate from law school. He proudly said, "Now I'm a judge!" The judge paused and his voice hushed. He concluded, "I'll never forget what you did for me."

I was taken aback. I never expected to see the Sergeant again or to receive such warm thanks for something that happened so long ago. It did make me realize that the little things we do can make a big difference in a life.

Sadly, I heard that Judge Riley died of a heart attack two years after our reunion. I will always remember him fondly, and I've told this story many times to my students, that they should be aware that their actions may be important to the future of their patients.

DID YOU KNOW TOM KELLEY?

id you know Tom Kelley? I had asked the question to a Vietnam veteran who had told me he had served on the River Boats. He paused before answering and then quietly replied that he did not know Tom Kelley, never met him, but he knew about him. Everyone in the boats knew about Tom Kelley, knew what he did. His voice trailed off and he didn't say anything else. His comments were delivered with such reverence that I was stunned. I had made the inquiry because I had read in a publication from my college, Holy Cross, that my classmate Thomas Kelley had been awarded the Congressional Medal of Honor for his actions while serving on the River Boats in Vietnam.

I realized I should know more about my fellow classmate of the Class of 1960 than I did. I went back to our school yearbook. There were four Kellies in my class, not unexpected for a Catholic college in New England. There in the senior section, between the photos of Kevin E. Kelley and Andrew J. Kelly, was a picture of a handsome, well-dressed young man named Thomas G. Kelley. The bio read that he was from Roxbury, Mass. He had received a bachelor of science degree in economics, his major field of study. He had participated in several extracurricular activities, including varsity hockey, several clubs, programs, and intramurals. He was the business manager for the yearbook.

As I was putting the book down, I noticed a large photograph tucked between the pages. It was a class photo taken at our tenth anniversary of graduation. We were at that time a bunch of young men confidently embarking on our careers. Dressed in the styles of the time, wide ties and colors, showing longish hair and sporting wide smiles. In the back of the group was one classmate in Navy dress-whites and wearing the insignia of lieutenant commander.

He was not smiling. His face was scarred and twisted. He was our man, Tom Kelley. I don't remember meeting Tom at that reunion. I had barely known him when we were both students. We had been taking different courses and engaged in different activities. In 1970, we were both Vietnam veterans, but I didn't make the connection. I wish we had spoken at that 1970 reunion; I would like to think I could have given him some encouragement in his battle with the terrible wounds he had suffered.

I did get to meet Tom in 2018 at a dinner of the O'Callahan Society, the organization for NROTC at Holy Cross. The society was named for Father O'Callahan who was a member of the Holy Cross faculty, and who had been awarded the Congressional Medal of Honor for his efforts to save the USS Franklin while serving in the Navy Chaplain Corps during the Second World War. I had only been in the ROTC Program for one year before changing my plans and switching to pre-med, but I was invited to join because I had served as an officer in the Navy.

Tom was the invited speaker for the event. He gave a nice talk about his love for the Navy. Despite his injuries and the loss of one eye, he served thirty years in the Navy and retired as a captain. He had been happily married to a female Navy officer who was a commander. After retirement, Tom served as the Commissioner of Veteran Affairs for the State of Massachusetts. After the dinner, I spoke with Tom for a while. He still bore the facial scars of his Vietnam injuries, but plastic surgery and the passing years had decreased the disfigurement that he exhibited in 1970. Tom told me he had always wanted to be a Navy officer. He had applied for Annapolis, but was rejected because of poor vision. He was rejected from NROTC for the same reason. After graduation from Holy Cross, he applied to Officer's Candidate School and was accepted. He finally realized his dream of becoming an officer in the United States Navy.

During his speech, and in our conversation, Tom never spoke about the action that earned him his award. He was very humble about his service, and he had praise for his enlisted men, especially for the corpsman who had braved enemy fire to address his wounds.

Curious about what actions were responsible for the medal, I turned to the Internet. A thorough description of the action was available. The narrative indicated that Lieutenant Thomas Kelley was leading a column of eight assault craft up the Ong Muong Canal on June 15, 1969. They were extracting a company of Army troops. One of the boats became disabled by a mechanical failure of the loading ramp. The disabled boat began receiving enemy fire from the opposite bank fifty meters away. Lt. Kelley ordered the other boats to circle the disabled boat and return fire. He positioned his boat directly in front of the malfunctioning boat. An enemy rocket knocked the lieutenant to the deck and caused him to have a severe head wound. Unable to stand, he relayed orders through one of his enlisted men, directing the disabled boat to raise the ramp manually and firing at the enemy until they withdrew.

The Medal of Honor citation noted that, "The lieutenant commander's brilliant leadership and bold initiative and resolute determination served to inspire his men and provided the impetus needed to carry out the mission. His extraordinary courage under fire and his selfless devotion to duty sustain and enhance the finest traditions of US Naval Service."

I was blown away by the account.

Did I know Tom Kelley? I didn't, but I am proud to say that I do now.

GOING BACK

I had an easier time in Vietnam than many. When I returned to complete my surgical training, I found that I was way ahead of my fellow residents in experience and maturity. I worked to complete my surgical training at Bellevue Hospital. Another great adventure! After residency, I established a successful private practice in orthopedic surgery. I also raised a family and I was a competitive runner and triathlete. Life was busy.

I did think about Vietnam more than about other parts of my life, but not obsessively, I believed. I stopped cringing every time I heard a helicopter landing. The time did come when my work tapered down, as it does when the kids grew up and went off on their own, as they do, and I had more time to think. What I thought about increasingly was Vietnam. I thought about my time there, my patients, the people I served with, and the suffering people of the country. I thought about my brother Nick who was one of two survivors of his original platoon.

I started looking on the Internet for the places where I had been or where my patients had fallen. One day, surfing the net, I came upon a site that asked, "Thinking about going back?" I stopped and thought about it. I had not been thinking about going back, but now, suddenly, I was. I had questions in my mind about what had happened to the beautiful, but troubled, nation and to the people I had barely come to know. The site was run by US military veterans who took fellow veterans back to the places where they had served. I was curious to see where my patients had been wounded; I knew the names, Khe San, Con Tien, The Rock Pile, Hill 806, and others. Those names appear on my military record as places where I had served, but I hadn't actually been to them.

After thinking things over one night, I said to my wife, "I'm thinking about going back to Vietnam."

Without hesitation, she replied, "You have to go back."

I was surprised at how well she understood how I felt. Thank God for that.

I did respond to Vietnam Battlefield Tours and started the process of preparation for the trip which would focus on Northern I Corps. The tour requested information from me about where I had been and what I would like to see. I received information about what to pack, what to expect, and where we would be going.

On March 8, 2015, my tour group met in the lobby of the Four Points Sheraton Hotel in Los Angeles. I shouldn't have been surprised we all looked older. Years had passed. Some veterans were alone, like me, and some were with their wives. All were anxious for the trip. Our leader was Marine SGT Bill Stilwagen who greeted the group and began to get us organized.

In a quiet moment, I asked Bill, "Who goes on these trips?"

He quickly replied, "Veterans who go on these tours are the guys who think about Vietnam every day of their lives."

I randomly asked three of my fellow tour goers, "How often do you think about Vietnam?"

All three quickly answered, "Every day of my life."

After an easy flight to Taipei, the group assembled in an empty waiting room where Bill gave us "The Talk;" a one-hour summary of what to expect in the new Vietnam and how to keep out of trouble. He included practical tips, like how to cross a street through heavy motorbike traffic.

2015 had seen a bitter cold winter in the East. I left home with two feet of snow on my property. Stepping out of our plane in Phu Bai, I was hit by a blast of warm, humid air. I had forgotten how hot Vietnam could be. Through the length of the trip, I continued to be drenched in perspiration.

The tour included overnight stays in Haoi, Hue, Dong Ha, Hoi An, and Da Nang. The accommodations were always comfortable and the food was great. We visited battlefields in Gio Lin, Camp Carrol, Con Thein, Khe Sanh Lang Vei, Hue, Razorback, and Hamburger Hill. One of the veterans had lost a leg in the battle for Hamburger Hill. He made the arduous climb up the hill using his prosthetic leg. There was no evidence of prior American presence at any of these sites. Whatever we built had vanished.

My first surprise occurred in Hanoi. Stepping out of our bus, I saw a line of young school kids walking past. Without any warning, I burst into tears. I suppose that some memory of the kids I had treated was aroused. Two of the wives on the trip quickly saw my distress and gave me comforting embraces. In the course of the trip, every one of us shed tears that had been suppressed for so many years.

The US Military kept very exact records of every action during the Vietnam conflict and our guides did extensive preparation to make the trip special for each veteran. With the GPS technology, it was possible to find where any event occurred.

One day, our bus stopped and our guides got out and chatted with some villagers. "Recon Bob," one of our veterans, joined them. They were looking for the place where Recon Bob had been wounded by a rocket in 1967. Our entire group left the bus and headed across the rice paddies, guided by a smiling former VC. We came to the location indicated by the GPS. Bob wasn't sure of the spot as the house was different than he remembered, but a neighbor joined us to say there had been remodeling done. Bob smiled at finding this place where his war ended.

Driving along the coast near Dong Ha, we stopped and Bill shouted, "Doc, what do you see?" I looked at the beach, the palm trees, and the South China Sea. It was the same view I had seen many times from the USS Repose. I remembered seeing fishing boats on the beach. One half-mile down the beach, the fishing boats were lined up as they were fifty years before.

When we came to a place where someone's friend had died, there were always tears from the whole group. That was the hardest thing.

Vietnam is a different place today. The battlefields are gone and hold different institutions. Our helicopter base in Phu Bai now has a Carlsberg brewery. Khe Sanh is the site of a coffee plantation that produces a great coffee. It also has a government museum about the battle of Khe Sanh with the most outrageous government lies imaginable, (e.g. the communists sank thirty American ships during the battle). The country has a young, friendly, and hard- working population. Virtually every Vietnamese speaks American English. The major currency is the US dollar. The people love Americans and hate the Chinese. Although the Communist Party is in power, only two percent of the population is communist. It was comforting to see that our worst fears about Vietnam did not come true and the people are becoming prosperous and happy.

On our last night in Da Nang, we had a more "formal" dinner in a luxurious restaurant. Each of us was asked to speak about our experience during the war. It was not easy for anyone. A ceremonial place was set for the "missing soldier." The following evening, we attended a reception in the US Embassy in Hanoi before flying home.

After returning home, I saw my neighbor, also a veteran, and told him that I had just come back from Vietnam. He replied he would never go back there, and he thinks about Vietnam "every day of my life."

I told my wife what Jeffrey had said, and she quietly enquired, "Do you think about Vietnam every day of your life?" After a moment, I replied that I did.

POPASMOKE

I received an E-mail from my friend, Rod, a veteran, who had been a helicopter pilot in Vietnam. He was asking if I had any recollection of a Marine operation that turned out badly in May,1967. He had received several E-Mails from members of his helicopter reunion group, popasmoke.com. The forwarded messages painted a grim picture of a Vietnam battlefield strewn with dead and wounded marines after their position was over-run by North Vietnamese troops. The helicopter units had the grim task of removing over one hundred bodies to Graves Registration and flying a large number of wounded marines to medical facilities, including the USS Repose, my hospital ship.

I immediately thought of a day in the spring of 1967 when the morning calm was shattered by a call for Flight Quarters, requesting all personnel to prepare for receiving ninety-six emergency medivacs. The number was way beyond anything that the Repose had handled before. I wondered if the message was a mistake. The entire ship's company scanned the skies and quickly noticed a very long string of helicopters approaching from the southwest and rapidly closing on our ship.

Calls continued ordering medical personnel to the triage area and litterbearers to the flight-deck. A boatload of divers was lowered into the water, preparing for any possible crash at sea. The fire suppression team was ready next to the flight-deck. The first UH-34 was already circling to land. The feeling of the repose crew was one of excitement and dread. We had a limited number of operating rooms, a limited number of surgeons, and a very limited number of anesthesia doctors. Wounded combatants had to be treated as expeditiously as possible if they were going to survive. Would this be the time that we would not be able to save all of our marines? I felt like the clock was ticking.

We all knew what had to be done. The wounded were carried into triage and evaluated, one at a time by members of the surgical team. Vital signs were recorded, injuries were documented and their severity noted. Then each patient was presented to Dr. Snyder, the Chief of Surgery and our triage officer. It was his task to decide the order of care for each marine and to assign the surgical teams. Patients with vascular injuries, active bleeding, or penetrating abdominal injuries were given first priority. Minor injuries and intra-cranial head wounds were assigned lower priorities. Somehow the triage officer was able to prioritize all ninety-six. By the time the process was completed, the first patients were already in surgery, having their injuries addressed. I finished examining my last patient and turned to Dr. Snyder for my next assignment. The doctor sternly gave me the order to sleep for four hours and then to report to O.R. number two to begin operating. It was not easy to sleep with all of the excitement, but, I knew that it was important to have enough fresh surgeons to complete our task.

Under Dr. Snyder's direction, the operating rooms were kept busy, around the clock for three days. He acted as the Ringmaster, using his crew as efficiently as possible. I can't recall how many surgeries that I performed or assisted in. The entire staff was kept occupied. It was hardest on the anesthesia staff because they were only three and there were three operating rooms that they had to service. They did take turns getting some sleep so that they could function safely. With limited ORs, turning the rooms over quickly was a priority. Everyone did everything possible to move things along smoothly. I witnessed Commander Larry Glass, on more than one occasion, mopping the operating room deck to save a few minutes. The corpsmen who were scrub techs had taken to sleeping in the ORs, rather than returning to their bunks. It happened that I was the last surgeon to finish on day three. Patient number ninety-six was a marine who had sustained a gunshot wound to his big toe. He had the tip of the toe amputated but didn't require anything else. His wound healed without infection, despite the long delay in treatment.

It is my recollection that all ninety-six patients survived. I relayed that information to Rod and he sent the news on to his Popasmoke friends. While we were in Vietnam, it was difficult to get follow-up information on operations that we were involved in. It struck me that this might be the first time, after fifty-three years, that these pilots would have heard that their difficult and dangerous medivac had saved the lives of a number of marines.

CPSIA information can be obtained
at www.ICGtesting.com
Printed in the USA
LVHW080841221021
701186LV00015B/765